THE ORIENTAL MISSIONARY SOCIETY world outreach includes work in twelve nations of Latin America, Asia, and Europe. This advancing team of more than 2000 missionary and national co-workers emphasizes direct evangelism (including many Every Creature Crusade teams on the road each day, radio, and literature evangelism), Bible training for Christian leadership on each field, and the establishment and encouragement of growing national churches in each nation. In the 71 years of this evangelical, interdenominational faith outreach, God has involved thousands like you in prayer and obedience to Christ's Great Commission. For further information write:

THE ORIENTAL MISSIONARY SOCIETY
Box A
Greenwood, Indiana 46142
U.S.A.

MY GOD JUST WENT BY!

by

B. H. PEARSON

MOODY PRESS

CHICAGO

ISBN: 0-8024-5685-5

Printed in the United States of America

To

that company of hardy and heroic missionaries—many of them anonymous—without whom there would be no story, whose tingling adventures for God would fill many a larger volume than this and whose love and loyalty will leave me always their debtor;

and to

that company of Colombian Christians who with their own blood have written a story of triumph not yet told;

I dedicate this,

that those who have not shared our laughter and our tears may believe and know that God is passing by in Colombia.

Winging my way into
the sun-flecked dawn—
If I should not return,
say not I'm gone;

If what I lived for
still lives on
In younger hearts,
it still is dawn.

B. H. P.

Contents

Foreword

THE STORY OF COLOMBIA is like a tapestry. As the masterpiece is woven, it is seen from the reverse side—dark, blurred, and incomplete. What was filled with foreboding in years of darkness in Colombia is now seen to have produced a beautiful pattern. In reproducing the story, the author has the master pattern before him in retrospect.

The threads of the tapestry are all the unsung valiants whose very anonymity, like the faith heroes of Hebrews 11:33-39, only further exalts the God who led His people through this modern wilderness experience.

However, the task of selection and placement of people and events in their proper relationship to the story requires an artistry anointed with discerning appreciation. No one could have been more eminently qualified for this than B. H. Pearson.

Those of us who worked closely by his side during the beginning years of the "twenty-five year epoch" watched the outflow of this great spirit. Rarely does one find a life that moves with such ease across the barriers and boundaries of cultural distinctions. We learned to call him "Uncle Ben," though to Colombians and missionaries who admired and respected his dignity and character he was also "Doctor" Pearson. All of us sensed his keen empathy for the deepest emotions of our hearts.

The marvelous metamorphosis of Colombia took twenty-five years to accomplish what we see today. Again, only a dynamic mind tuned to history and contemporary movements could unite it all into a harmonious whole.

Almost all missionary chronicles reflect some specific field, work, or ministry. In this case the slant is toward the history of the Inter-American Missionary Society (the Latin American division of the Oriental Missionary Society). This should not distract the reader from seeing the glorious reality of Christ's body in its function and fullness. The IMS has been related to the fashioning of that body in a unique sense.

It is impossible to telescope the complete panorama into this small volume. A wealth of testimony lies untapped. We personally have listened by the hour to missionaries and nationals as they have recounted thrilling chapters of the untold story.

But, here is the open window looking out upon a corner of the great harvest field, where reapers still are busy gathering abundant fruit these days for the garners of God.

WILLIAM A. GILLAM

Oriental Missionary Society

PROLOGUE

The Call

From the pen and heart of Mrs. Charles E. Cowman, author of Streams in the Desert, *comes the account of the call through which the Inter-American Missionary Society was founded in Latin America.*

A very definite call from God came to me on Sunday morning, October 26, 1942. I had not had such guidance from the Lord in forty-two years!

I had gone to a quiet room in a small hotel at Winona Lake, supposedly to write. But I could not write. A burden and travail was laid upon me that lasted for weeks. I *saw* South America reaching out her hands of need. I *heard* her cry for help.

With this call which was as definite as that of forty-two years ago when we followed Him into the lands of the Far East, the prayer was made daily, almost hourly, "Lord, show us who will go with us into the lands of the Southern Cross."

I stood before a fast-barred door. Its hinges seemed rusted, and there was no power to move them. Oft' I was tested almost to the breaking point by the Lord's apparent leisureliness.

At last the still small voice was heard, "Up! For this is the day. I have set before thee an open door. Arise and enter it now for Me."

1

My God Just Went By!

WHAT A DISCOVERY! It seemed impossible! How could it be!

On a distribution map of churches and missions in Colombia, I had found big white spaces. These represented areas of Colombia in the department of Antioquia as yet unoccupied by evangelical forces. In this most populous region, the white spaces were inexplicable and mysterious. Medellin, the capital of the department, was the second largest city in the nation, and noted for textile industries. This seemed a likely place to enter.

But why? Why had such a prosperous part of Colombia been neglected by evangelical missions? Were Christian workers or missionaries not available? By what divine providence had this territory been left open until the year 1940?

I sat pondering this in my cabin on a steamship which lay at anchor in the port of Buenaventura, Colombia. The old rust-covered town looked down upon the quiet lagoons of the inner harbor. The projected journey would take me to most of South America, but the map on the table before me was exciting and kindled a desire to visit Medellin. Such a side trip was now impossible, for it would require a day's journey by bus, and the boat left in the morning.

Thereafter, however, Medellin and the department of Antioquia were recurring themes for meditation and prayer.

I had regarded two previous decades of work in Mexican missions as preparation for South America. Strange paradox: the election which removed me from Spanish-speaking missions had sent me on this journey.

After the return from South America, the pull of the south was so strong that I resigned my general church office to go into the lands of the Southern Cross. But resignations must be accepted to set one free. As mine was refused, I found myself with the same responsibilities as before. I presented a second, more urgent resignation, but without result. My soul, however, was quieted by what seemed the divine assurance, "This is a time of transition. Do with your might what your hand finds to do. I have the answer. It will not tarry."

Very soon I saw that God was weaving a pattern. First, there came a chance meeting with Mrs. Charles E. Cowman. Later I found in her writings these words, "It chanced—but God that chance did guide."

The rejection of my two resignations, which I had presented to go to South America under the missionary board of my denomination, answered completely the question as to why I applied to the Oriental Missionary Society. I was accepted immediately.

Shortly thereafter, at Winona Lake, Indiana, where Mrs. Cowman was making her temporary home, I met a most unusual young man and his charming wife—Bill and Mary Gillam. Mrs. Cowman had resided so long in Japan, with long stays in England, that afternoon tea, like morning prayers, became a ritual. On one such afternoon of fellowship, the Gillams and the Pearsons were brought together.

When Bill sat down at the piano to play in his free, inimitable style and then began to sing, I knew he was a natural for Latin lands. I could only hope that a man of Bill's personality and abilities might be my companion to South America.

As Mrs. Pearson and I went through the delightful and exhausting thrill of pulling loose from the US in preparation for travel to South America, the mystery persisted. How could an area so populous, so rich in industry, so advanced in culture as the department of Antioquia still have relatively little evangelical mission work? Why were *we* privileged to discover it? We could hardly wait to arrive.

Not only did we feel the call of God but, because we spoke Spanish, God doubtless discovered in our assurance of success some rather brash confidence, not to say human bravado.

We found that the door of entrance to Colombia was not easily opened. I spent the better part of a day chatting in Spanish with an older Colombian consul; as long as he kept talking, there was hope. Toward evening I saw that God was answering prayer: The consul visaed our passports. All three of us—my wife, Emma; our daughter, Esther Elizabeth; and I—were free to go.

By the unpredictable accidents of wartime travel, our family arrived in Medellin August 13, 1943. Below us, in the bright morning sunlight, shone the white walls and red-tiled roofs of Medellin, like something out of *Arabian Nights.* We saw the city, hidden so securely in this deep fold of the towering Andes, surrounded by green sunlit grass, mottled with dark clumps of semitropical shrubs, and a few scattered farms.

Medellin was no upstart metropolis: it was founded by

Mariscal Robledo in A.D. 1616. For three hundred years it had remained largely secluded from the outside world. Only recently the granite ramparts of the sheltering Andes had been pierced. The first train service to this valley had begun only fourteen years before our arrival. The first airplane did not land at the airport until July 5, 1932. We were little more than a decade away from arriving by donkey train and muleback!

Eight days later we welcomed Bill and Mary Gillam, and their two wee daughters, Judy and Linda. Ours was a joyous reunion. The warmhearted hospitality of Sterl Phinney and Bob Crosby of the Wesleyan Mission in receiving our two families temporarily into their homes was reassuring.

Just because he did not know Spanish was no reason for Bill to remain idle. He was besieged to play and lead the singing at evangelistic services beginning the Sunday night following his arrival. He protested, "I don't know a word of Spanish." But I assured him that there are only five vowels in Spanish with only one sound each. All he had to do was to sing the syllables of Spanish hymns, like Italian do-re-mi! It was a tour de force that few men could have attempted, and fewer could have brought off so successfully.

The music of his accordion was a universal language, and all Colombians understood at once Bill's warm, contagious smile. He came through the ordeal as though this was his regular Sunday evening program. Bill said afterward that playing the accordion and trying to sing in Spanish never more than one syllable away from disaster left him trembling with exhaustion. But he did it. He had broken the "sound barrier." Never again would he be terrified by this beautiful language. Only an impossible challenge can demonstrate a man's capacity.

Bill and Mary were fortunate to find in Medellin a splendid language school under the direction of the Presbyterian mission. It was located in Medellin because of the ideal climate and the city's cultural importance. Missionaries on their way to all parts of Latin America came here. The Gillams not only enrolled for study, but made lasting friendships with these future evangelical leaders of South America, some of whom were destined for the missionary hall of fame. Already it was becoming difficult to secure visas for students. Later, even temporary permission to enter for study was denied; and by 1950, the language school was forced to close in Medellin but reopened in Costa Rica.

The task of finding living quarters for our two families was little less than an adventure. Fear of social pressure kept many from renting to us. Attitudes of the monolithic society about us placed Protestants, Communists, heretics, Freemasons, and all other deviates from Colombian traditionalism in a single dubious category!

Finally we made friends with Rafael Torres, two hundred fifty pounds of pleasant, dynamic, hearty, puffing, nonsuspicious *Antioqueño* realtor. Fortunately the ambivalence in Antioquian character due to an avid interest in American dollars was highly developed in him! He never permitted sectarian scruples to intrude into business relations: he was just too big to have qualms about a little thing like religion! Of course he would find us a house—a good one, the kind "foreigners" like, the kind that would be just right for people engaged in "your kind of business." Though he thus alluded gently to our surreptitious character, he was just man enough to overlook it.

Less than a month later, Mr. Torres called with hopeful mien to guide us to a place on "La Avenida" (The Avenue). From the time he unlocked the front wrought-iron gate and we started down a walled corridor past "houses" on either side, we felt a tingle of excitement.

This place *was* different. The passageway brought us to a large covered patio, open on two sides. On the far side of this patio (an unbelievable sight!), we saw the dark green of a heavy grass lawn, some sixty or seventy feet wide and fifty feet long. How good it felt to tramp on a real lawn once more. Facing the lawn along one side of the house was a covered tile terrace.

It was an old-fashioned country home, now engulfed by the growing city. This ancient house was of *tapia* construction, common in the colonial period—large earthen blocks, thick enough to keep out the heat, plastered over with *revoque* made by mixing mud and manure, but smooth, and painted a lovely cheerful yellow. The building was two stories high at one end, with large airy rooms throughout, plenty of double doorways, and, in addition to the covered patio, two other patios open to the sky—ideal for a first headquarters. Visitors gasped in astonishment at sight of the lawn and asked, "How did you find this? Did you search for it with an airplane?"

No manual on missions recommends this, but since Bill and Mary Gillam were not yet at home in Spanish, we unanimously decided that for now our two families would live together in the house on La Avenida. Bill, assisted by his remarkable musical ear and aural memory, mastered Spanish rapidly. He became not only a gifted public speaker in the language, but a composer of Spanish hymns that captivated the Latin heart and are still being sung throughout South America.

One day Sterl Phinney said, "Would you like to see where another mission tried to establish a beachhead?"

We jumped into his car and drove along a street that had been notched in the side of the valley. The roofs of houses on the lower side were about level with the roadway. Sterl stopped the car above a neat clean building and said, "That's the place. That's where they started their work in Antioquia. It wasn't long until mobs formed, and that building was under a hail of rocks and stones. The filth thrown and the general harassment were such that they abandoned Medellin and this department. However, they're doing well in another part of Colombia."

He did not have to say more. The mission to which Mr. Phinney referred had a record of success in some of the toughest mission fields in the world. If they could not succeed here, how could we? Had we sold ourselves a rock farm, where gospel seed would not produce a harvest? Had God lured us here for some special discipline? Was what this other mission suffered a prophecy of our future? This was a sobering thought. Now we thought we understood why so little evangelical work could be found in this department of Antioquia.

Thus, understanding of the mystery began, but yet a greater and more difficult question emerged: how could we succeed where a mission of such prestige had apparently failed?

Gradually any illusory or romantic preconceptions of mission work in Antioquia gave way to reality.

Yes, we knew we faced a difficult task. Yet, an anecdote shared with us by Sterl Phinney reminded us of our reasons for coming to Antioquia.

Sterl told us that one day, a small red automobile, for all the world like a piece of fire-fighting equipment, drove up the street ringing a clanging bell. As the maid who was working for the Phinneys heard the sound, she rushed to the window, dropped to her knees—eyes wide and staring heavenward—then crossed herself and clasped her hands in supplication.

When Mrs. Phinney asked her why, she answered, "My God just went by!"

This red car with the bell sounding so loudly was taking Holy Communion to a dying man. No wonder people stopped, men's hats came off, many dropped to their knees, all crossed themselves. For them, the consecrated Host—the Eucharistic wafer—that rode past was the body, person, passion, and sacrifice of Christ. What would *you* do if you really believed that the eternal God, Jesus Christ, Creator of all worlds, our Lord and Saviour was riding down the street in a red automobile?

Thinking this over, my mind went back centuries, as God, in the person of Jesus, once "passed by."

Could He do it again?

In Antioquia?

Could He be so glorified here that men would say of the living Christ, "God just went by"?

If He didn't, we were sunk!

If He did, He, and He alone, would be forever glorified.

2

First Christmas

Before our first Colombia Christmas came, Miss Edna Evans joined our missionary family and began using her journalistic expertise in editing and publishing *Aurora* (dawn), a Christian magazine bequeathed to us by the Cumberland Presbyterians. Also Robert Neighbor, Jr., a well-known violinist was with us.

Something very strange for Christmastime aroused our curiosity. At irregular intervals, at almost any hour of the day or night, a sound like the blast of exploding bombs echoed and reverberated up and down the streets. Was some sort of violence in the air? Perhaps a revolution getting under way?

No, not at all! The sound came from young and old setting off giant firecrackers to herald the approach of the feast of the Immaculate Conception, celebrated on December 8. This commemorated the Roman Catholic dogma of the sinless conception of the Virgin Mary to preserve her free from sin as a pure vessel for the incarnation of our Saviour.

The holy day had scarcely passed, when one of our number rushed back from the business center of Medellin bringing the most fantastic story: merchants were closing their stores! He had seen them deliberately putting up heavy iron grills and wooden shutters, and locking their doors. It seemed a huge joke; it couldn't be! We *knew* it couldn't be! What? Close your store two weeks before Christmas! Except for a coup d'etat or an invasion, only madmen would do that. For businessmen who loved money as they did, it was impossible!

Further inquiry confirmed the news. Store proprietors refused to be cheated out of their personal Christmas holidays. Most of them had little country homes thousands of feet higher in the Andes, or down in the hot river areas. To change their elevation was the only way possible for those living so near the equator to change their climate. (In Colombia the height above sea level where you live determines the year-round season that will be yours—from springtime flowers to winter snows.)

These proprietors turned the locks in their doors with an air of holiday relief that many a merchant prince of the United States might have envied! Instead of festive Christmas decorations, lights, and Santa Clauses, downtown Medellin would be a desert of drab and darkened stores.

One thing was clear: only an immediate and frantic Christmas buying foray could keep us from famine. It was not a question of turkey and cranberry sauce, just a matter of having enough food for the table three times a day. How long would the stores be closed? And presents—what about presents? We must act at once; the spoils would go to the swift!

Later, upon returning from the shopping area, we held a conclave to compare purchases. Robert Neighbor, Jr., the tall, long-armed violinist, made the most exciting buy. In the one store he found open, the only likely Christmasy purchase was an assortment of roller skates. As shutters were slamming into place, he dare not haggle over prices nor look further. He bought them all—four pair!

Robert had no wrapping paper, nor time to wrap them and put on the package a nice little card saying, "Hold till Christmas!" It was all unplanned and spontaneous. He just came in, laughing hilariously at himself, with those roller skates dangling over his shoulder.

Perhaps it was the violent awakening to the nearness of Christmas, or it may have been a reaction to the unrelenting pressures under which the group lived and worked, but it was astonishing to see nearly everyone grab for those skates.

The house on La Avenida was admirably adapted to what happened next. From its sixty-foot hallway, one could shoot out onto the tiled porch or terrace and then zoom back to the large covered patio. Nearly everybody, young or old, excitedly buckled on one or two of the skates and started careening around the place, shouting, laughing, arms flailing in the air, spills imminent, grabbing doorjambs to make sharp turns; and woe betide him or her who failed to remember the skating "pattern." The pent-up emotions of past months were released in delightful merriment. It was a riotous time; no one could have planned such a Christmas as the one that burst upon us.

Gradually the tempo and volume of firecracker explosions increased toward a veritable crescendo.

Globos were another peculiarity of this 1943 Medellin Christmas. *Globos* are homemade tissue-paper balloons, four to six feet tall, and often as big around as an old-fashioned barrel. At the lower end, or mouth, of the *globo*, a rag previously soaked in gasoline is tied to a wire frame and ignited. The hot air sweeps these contraptions up into the sky for a tremendous voyage around the valley. They would zigzag back and forth over the city in the changing air currents, like so many Unidentified Flying Objects. Tile roofs and brick construction made them relatively harmless. Crowds of youngsters sought to catch them as they fell, to start them on another journey. Whether by day or by night, their bright colors added an unusual gala aspect to the valley.

Even the daily newspaper caught the *Antioqueño* Christmas spirit. On December 20 an announcement appeared, boxed in red, wishing all readers a "Happy Christmas" and a "Prosperous New Year." The statement added that the next issue of the paper would be on January 6!

That really was a shocker! Not only was business at a standstill, not only were proprietors, managers, and workers on a long holiday, but—come wars or financial crashes, revolutions or the fall of kings and governments—the public was not to have their Christmas joy disturbed by news! So be it! This was a new version of "Peace on earth, goodwill to men"; something so original and intriguing that perhaps only the citizens of this 5,000-foot valley, hidden behind 10,000-foot mountains and higher peaks, could have dreamed it up or had the nerve to do it.

Christmas, blessed Christmastime! Equatorial Christmas in the summertime! But Christmas—a time to get away from traffic jams and ceaseless bargaining, out into the freshness of grass and trees and purling streams. The commercial part of Medellin might die temporarily, but families together enjoyed the simple pleasures of long walks through the country, or telling long stories by starlight or candlelight. Who cared about the worthless bagatelle of profits from pre-Christmas shopping days!

And why not? I wonder if they did not have much to teach us. Yes, and to teach the Medellin of today that has permitted the mercantile Christmas pattern of North America to replace its own easygoing holiday traditions.

In those quiet halcyon days of yesteryear, one could think, almost with pity, of friends in the United States frantically working long hours on cards not yet sent, or on last-minute buying splurges that lasted till the stores closed on Christmas Eve.

As we sat in the warm summer sun of a Colombian Christmas, we felt grateful for the quiet restfulness of a city muted (save for an occasional firecracker), and for families enjoying together the peacefulness of quiet country spots under the trees, by gently flowing streams, or cooled by the white spray of waterfalls.

During these delightful days we could not have imagined that in a few months the courage and fortitude of our number would be tested by a baptism of fire.

3

Prelude to Violence

AFTER CHRISTMAS and New Years, the commercial heart of Medellin came to life gradually. This followed no pattern; stores opened when the owner returned from his vacation. It was as simple as that!

One store that specialized in needed building materials not obtainable elsewhere, remained closed for so long that we sought to discover what had happened. An acquaintance informed us, "That man made so much money before Christmas, he will not have to open until March or April!"

Well, why not? In the New Testament we read, "A man's life consisteth not in the abundance of the things which he possesseth" (Lk 12:15). Granted that the attitude of the Colombian people was more hedonistic than Christian, yet, we are warned not to let life become "choked with cares and riches."

The somewhat idyllic episode of our first Christmas might beguile you into thinking that we were in a new-found Eden. But Medellin is the capital of the department of Antioquia, which ruthlessly proud Spaniards conquered in the days of the conquistadores. Because they "solved the Indian problem by liquidating these aborigines," because Basque and Jewish settlers followed, because gold mining fomented "Wild West" attitudes, or because for centuries they were shut away from the outside world, the people of this department became a fiercely independent "race" that considered themselves a different "breed" from the rest of Colombia. Here men killed and were killed for politics, for religion, or for that elusive thing called "the point of honor."

Nothing could have seemed a more innocuous beginning of adventure than for Sterl Phinney to ask assistance in starting a Sunday school. He planned it for La Union, a small but centrally located trading center that served the plateau extending southward above the valley of Medellin. If the rule held true that the greater the elevation the greater the resistance to change, this place would not be easy to penetrate. But it was important to establish a gospel anchor point in this populous highland.

One sunny Sunday morning, under white clouds that poured down light as well as occasional showers, an automobile carrying a small group started for the first service in La Union. After a climb of several thousand feet up the winding mountain road on the southern side of the Medellin valley, the travelers found themselves above the clumps of cottony clouds that help maintain the perpetual springtime of Medellin.

As they crossed the rim of the valley, the road dipped slightly toward the rolling plains that form the high Andean plateau beyond the town of Rio Negro. On either side were verdant pastures, broken by clumps of uncleared jungle. A narrow river flowed silently along a channel whose banks seemed landscaped to fit the terrain. Humble dwellings indicated small *fincas* (farms) where owners lived and worked the land. More sumptuous places were evidently vacation spots for wealthy families, with saddle horses in the pasture.

When the Christian workers arrived at the outskirts of

La Union, Sterl Phinney parked his car beside the rock curbing in front of a small country home. It appeared to be about one and one-half stories high. An adobe wall enclosed the property. The house, built of *tapia,* was set back approximately twenty feet from the narrow dirt sidewalk.

The man of the house who had expressed a willingness for Bible reading and teaching in his home appeared shortly, unlocked a heavy chain, swung open the gate, and in the taciturn way of the country people of the high Andes, bade the group enter; then he led the way upstairs to a rustic room with very low ceiling. In a few moments his wife appeared. Soon two or three men climbed the narrow stairs, entered, and slid silently into one of the *tabaretes* (wooden frames upholstered with cowhides).

All listened to the Bible reading and explanation with expressionless faces. They showed neither interest nor hostility, just the cold, close-lipped attitude of people who live in the lonely Andean heights. After the service, the few listeners walked out as silently as they had come.

The Medellin-Sonson road ran through La Union connecting it with the outside world. In front of the house in which the Bible studies were held, this road narrowed, making a U-turn impossible. The return trip required driving down to the plaza, and—despite crowds of bargain hunters, vendors' stalls, and crowds of children—turning around and heading back to Medellin.

As Sunday visits to the home continued, three to eight people would come for the Bible messages. Even these small gatherings marked a daring thrust for the first time into this high Andean territory.

When work elsewhere hindered those who usually conducted these Sunday morning services, Bill Gillam was asked to become responsible. He welcomed the opportunity to use his newly acquired Spanish and to become better acquainted with Colombians. Benigno Mantilla, a soft-spoken, courageous Latin preacher, and Jose Gutierrez, a zealous, daring witness accompanied Bill in a brown Plymouth loaned for the trip. This was Bill's first experience of conducting a Sunday service on his own.

This particular morning, when the three men reached La Union, the owner of the house where the Bible class met apologized for having forgotten his keys. However, as a group of stolid, silent men began gathering around the automobile, interest seemed higher than ever. Bill said later, "I had to have a street meeting or nothing. I was very naïve about street meetings in Colombia. The two Christians workers with me were for it."

Bill got out his accordion, and he and his two companions stood on the sidewalk and began singing. Before long, on the edge of the gathering, Bill noticed a well-dressed man beckoning to him. Realizing that he could not yet speak Spanish sufficiently to converse easily with this stranger, Bill asked Jose Gutierrez to talk to him.

In a moment Jose reported, "This man is the mayor of La Union. He says that this morning in church the priest denounced us from the pulpit."

Bill asked, "What did the mayor recommend?"

Jose replied, "He says that it would be better for us to close the street meeting and get out of here before something happens."

"What do you think we should do?"

"This is a free country," Jose answered emphatically. "The constitution of Colombia guarantees freedom of worship. We should go right ahead with this service."

Benigno Mantilla had begun a brief message on the love of God. All was quiet. The crowd seemed to be listening attentively. When Beningo finished, the three men sang a chorus. Apparently it was a triumph.

As Bill opened the car door to leave, someone yelled, "*Abajo los Protestantes!* [Down with the Protestants!] *Viva la Virgen!* [Long live the Virgin!]" Rocks flew past the heads of the three men and crashed into the wall behind them. Rocks began to crash against the car.

Bill's first thought was for the preservation of the automobile, as it was not mission property. Quickly, he shoved the accordion into the car, and the three men jumped in. Never before had Bill driven a vehicle under such adverse circumstances. As best he could, he began edging the car slowly through the crowd and on down the narrow street toward the plaza. He had to reach that plaza to turn around. He had to reach that plaza! He *had* to!

Inside the car the tattoo of rock against glass and metal made a continuous din. The safety glass of windows and windshield cracked, threatening to give way. A few men began pounding the car fenders and body with huge wooden clubs. Occasionally a man would attempt to tip the car over. Bill knew that they had to keep moving, but to run down a man would have turned the crowd into a killing frenzy.

To drive that block down to the plaza and turn the car around despite the throng of morning shoppers and the attack of the mob was the only possible escape. It was never easy to turn around in the plaza; it would be impossible today. Rocks were beginning to smash through the windows and come inside the car.

As the car moved slowly through the weird, wild scene of the plaza—women scurrying, dogs barking, horses rearing, donkeys pulling at their tethers; men, women, and children shouting; stones smashing into the car—Jose Gutierrez yelled at Benigno, who sought to restrain him, "Let me out! Let me out! I want out! I'm getting out!"

Bill shouted, "You can't do that, Jose! Stay in! They will kill you!"

Wrenching himself free from Benigno, Jose jumped to the ground.

What Jose Gutierrez did diverted attention away from the car. It was possible to drive on through the remaining hazards of stalls, tables, animals, and shouting people. Afterward, Bill remarked, "It was a miracle that we did not kill someone."

As the car came out of the plaza onto the road for home, the crowd fell away, and it was possible to increase speed.

As Bill Gillam and Benigno Mantilla looked back, they could see the mob surrounding Jose. It seemed that he had chosen martyrdom: he was giving his life to save theirs. Jose's action could be interpreted in no other way except that he was willing to die to save a gringo missionary and a Latin American preacher of brief acquaintance.

Could it be that he had actually demonstrated what Jesus calls the greatest love of all?

When Bill arrived in Medellin with the wrecked car, people stared in disbelief. The exterior appeared totally destroyed. But the principal concern was for the fate of Gutierrez. The missionaries had one powerful option—united prayer for his safe return. It seemed impossible, yet "all things are possible to him that believeth."

Late that afternoon, an unwounded and unharmed Jose calmly walked in. He told a story of deliverance as fantastic as his apparently rash act of stepping out into the mob at La Union. Rocks thrown at him had missed and crashed into the mob surrounding him, wounding eleven men so severely that they had to be taken on a truck to the clinic in the city of La Ceja.

The mayor, who was also the chief of police, then rushed in and placed Jose under protective custody. After taking him to the city hall, a noisy, yelling crowd gathered outside, demanding that Jose be turned over to them. The town was in an uproar. Jose was a person of most independent thought. He trusted God and he trusted himself as a son of God. Jose not only had faith in God, he was also a worthy son of Antioquia. Born and reared in these Andes, he instinctively knew the psychology of his people. To hide behind the civil power of the police, did not fit the norm by which he lived. He knew his people despised weakness and admired strength. He determined to defy the mob in a final gesture and risk all on it. Whatever happened to him, his Lord would be glorified among this people.

When Jose finally overcame the mayor's reluctance and stepped through the suddenly opened door of the city hall, the throng of men silently parted before him and let him through.

On the outskirts of the town he took a bus. The missionaries that day rated Jose the bravest and most daring man they ever met.

4

Manantiales Miracle

MUCH WAS HAPPENING in Medellin. That meant problems. Problems are the why of missions! No problems, no missions! A missionary revels in problems—the right kind of problems. Problems are what put him in his field, and problems are what keep him there. The more problems, the more progress—providing God solves the problems. As God solves problems, bigger and better ones emerge. A mission is a continuing series of problems and solutions—solutions and problems!

Bill Gillam, who started out singing one syllable at a time, was now in demand across Colombia for conventions and evangelistic services. Young people began saying to him, "Won't you teach me the Bible?" Or, "God has called me to preach. Where can I study?" One of these was a highly educated young man who, before his escape from Hitler, had led a large Christian movement of German youth.

Now that Bill and Mary had moved out of the mission headquarters on La Avenida, their former apartment was turned into a young men's dormitory, and the students ate on the rear terrace. Classes were held in a nearby mission chapel. More problems, more blessings! In the anticipation of faith, Bill wrote the first prospectus for the Bible

Seminary of Colombia. By the time directors of the mission caught up with us, we had ten students.

The directors, Rev. Edwin ("Bud") Kilbourne and Rev. Harry Woods, appeared in Medellin on June 3, 1945. E. A. Kilbourne, cofounder of the mission, had taken his son, Bud, to Japan at an early age. Harry was one of the famed "Ten," a group of Bible students who volunteered to go to Japan in 1917 to complete history's first Every Creature Crusade. Together these ten young men walked fifty thousand miles in one year to reach the homes of Japan with the gospel. Both directors came recently from concentration camps in China where they had been engulfed by the invading Japanese armies. We didn't hold our breath, but who could keep from wondering what judgment these men might form on our new venture in a culture so remote and so different as the department of Antioquia, Colombia?

To our delight, their zest and enthusiasm inspired us with an even greater vision. They decided to make Medellin, Colombia, the mission's first headquarters in South America; also to approve the meager teaching schedule already begun and to purchase a permanent site for the seminary.

Search as we might, we could find no suitable place. Even if owners had not asked exorbitant prices, we had no money with which to buy the right accommodations.

On the morning of June 10, after scripture reading, Bud Kilbourne, the senior member of the party, said to Harry Woods, "Harry, yesterday you told the Bible class that the Holy Spirit in our day is just like Jesus was for His disciples. He guides us as Jesus guided them. Now, we must have His guidance to find the right place for our seminary. We don't have sense enough to find it, and if we did, we might not recognize it. Let's get on our knees and ask the

Holy Spirit to lead us at once to the place God has chosen for us."

Harry is a quiet man, and he protested mildly, "Now, Bud, you mustn't carry that too far."

But Bud Kilbourne broke in, "That's what you preached, Harry, and I believe it. Let's get on our knees and ask God to do it." With that he dropped to his knees, as did the others. His prayer was as direct and blunt as his previous statement. When he finished the brief prayer, all stood up with an air of expectancy. We felt God was going to answer—*had* answered. We did not have long to wait.

Previously, our Colombian realtor friend, Rafael Torres, had been consulted. So many days had gone by without a word from him that we thought we might have become "hot cargo," and he might not wish to be involved in such an undertaking.

To our complete surprise, within thirty minutes after Bud Kilbourne's prayer, our rotund realtor came puffing up to the locked wrought-iron gate on La Avenida, calling for admittance. He seemed elated as he announced loudly, "I think I have the property you are looking for. Los Cerritos estate, owned by Dr. Luis Escarpetta."

Kilbourne, Woods, Gillam, and I climbed into Torres' automobile to drive through the morning traffic jam of pedestrians, donkeys, horse carts, and automobiles which snarled Medellin's narrow streets, then on across the valley and up the northern slope past the School of Mines of Antioquia University. Never before had we considered or visited this side of the valley. Soon we were some hundreds of feet above the floor of the valley on what, even then, was known as the Pan-American Highway—largely a dream to be realized in future decades. Beautiful homes were all about us.

After a bit, the car turned up a steep rock and gravel country road, and through a large gate into a breathtakingly beautiful country estate. We drove around a large circle of gorgeous rose bushes in full bloom and stopped before a palatial residence. The modern architecture was enhanced by red and purple climbing bougainvillea in full bloom. On a huge granite outcropping, which we later named "The Rock of Ages," were growing clumps of dazzling orchids. Looking out above the trees in the garden below us, we saw Medellin's red-tiled rooftops against the upward surge of the southern wall of the valley, a backdrop rising to ten thousand feet above sea level. We almost gasped. This could not be for us!

As we were shown the large ten-room house, with four baths, situated in landscaped grounds of some three acres, we were like schoolboys exploring our first treasure island. We shouted and gesticulated until Bud said, "We'd better stop this. I'm afraid the price has doubled."

But it hadn't. The owner, Dr. Escarpetta, a government engineer, had left for another assignment. His wife remained to make the sale, which included the three acres of land, the beautiful home with all the furnishings, except a movable liquor bar and a marble statue of the Virgin Mary, which we graciously permitted them to take! For an immediate cash sale, the price was unbelievably under the market value.

There was just one catch: we had no cash!

The location was ideal, with room for expansion. We had found nothing to compare with it. The price was less and the value more than anything we had seen previously. Bud's prayer was answered—if we only had the money! This could not wait. Time was of the essence. However, we did have sufficient faith to ask for another day in which to arrange finances. To this, a gracious Mrs. Escarpetta assented.

Finding the property was one miracle. Could there be another? How would—or could—God work this out? It was wartime. Censorship delayed letters or cables for a week or more. The only human source of funds was the Los Angeles office of the Society. But, at least, the record would show that we tried. We dispatched an urgent cable to Mrs. Cowman and claimed whatever miracle was necessary to make the property ours.

The two veteran directors, Kilbourne and Woods, felt that we should make doubly sure by examining other possible sites. But the more properties we saw during the day, the more thrilled and excited we became about the Los Cerritos estate. We were so busy we did not even go for our mail. We could—and did—continue praying for a miracle.

The next morning when we went to the mission airmail box as usual, a surprise awaited us. Among the letters came one from Mrs. Cowman, written and mailed approximately ten days before. It may have been there the very morning we discovered the property. Her letter read:

"God spoke to me this morning. He said, 'Empty the treasury. Send it to Colombia.' I do not know what this money is to be used for. I am sure He will make it clear to you when it arrives."

Accompanying the letter were four checks for five thousand dollars each. When exchanged for Colombian pesos, we made cash payment for the property, paid all expenses of the transfer of title, and had enough to move the seminary operation to the new site. By the following day, June 12, the deal was completed, and the question forever answered. Yes, God did want us to locate in Medellin, the capital of Antioquia.

An irate neighbor who had wanted the property but had not known it was for sale said, "You didn't pay for that property. If you bought the land, the house was a gift; if you bought the house, the land was a gift!"

The money so miraculously sent came from the financial arrangement the mission had with Mrs. Cowman concerning her famous devotional book, *Streams in the Desert.* She gave the book to the mission, receiving no royalties from its sale, but the mission placed the profits from the book in a special fund that she could invest at will in any approved mission project.

Miss Frances L. Black, the mission's acting secretary-treasurer, later told this story: "That morning, Mrs. Cowman came into the office singing, cheerful and joyous as always. She said to me, "Frances, this morning God told me to empty the *Stream's* treasury and send it all to Colombia. Will you get the checks ready?'

"Usually, I accepted Mrs. Cowman's suggestion as the voice of the Lord; but the balance in this fund was now so large, I felt surely she must have missed her guidance. I went through the morning without writing the checks, feeling that by noon Mrs. Cowman would decide not to mention it again.

"At the noon hour, however, Mrs. Cowman came gaily past my desk, as she asked, 'Oh, Frances, are the checks ready?'

"I had to tell her, 'No, Mrs. Cowman. But I will have them for you immediately after lunch.' "

Mrs. Cowman's call established the Inter-American Mission in Latin America; her certainty of guidance and God's timing in sending the funds founded the seminary in Medellin.

From the high Andean range above us, a purling mountain stream ran through the seminary property; also, the book *Streams in the Desert* had furinshed the money, so the seminary grounds were renamed *Manantiales* (streams).

The name also expressed our faith that streams of living water from the lives of students and graduates would flow forth over Colombia and South America.

5

God's Timing

BEAUTIFUL MANANTIALES was far from being a seminary. To be a seminary it needed classrooms, dormitories, offices, a dining room, kitchen, and residence for teachers, not to mention a chapel and a library.

As excitement over the miraculous provision of the property subsided, the mission began facing up to required building tasks. Bill Gillam's deft hands drafted a beautifully designed administration building, but who would build it?

Seldom have missionaries taken courses in erecting three-story brick and concrete buildings on rough terrain in foreign lands! But the way in which God gave us Manantiales made it easy to believe that He had a plan for completing what He had begun.

The answer was already in South America. John Palmer and his wife, Beatrice, after graduating from the Birkenhead Bible School in England, had spent eleven years without furlough as missionaries in The Green Hell—El Chaco, that vast jungle area surrounded by Paraguay, Argentina, Chile, and Brazil. Their work included pioneering among Indians, evangelizing Spanish-speaking regions, and organizing building operations. John was ready for anything from deadly snakebite and attempted assassination to diplomatic encounters with heads of government.

Like many another missionary, John and Beatrice had a lifelong admiration for Mr. and Mrs. Charles E. Cowman. *Streams in the Desert* had been their devotional reading, and their lives had been molded by another book written by Mrs. Cowman, *Charles E. Cowman: Missionary Warrior.* It was but natural that, when they heard of "The Cowman-Kilbourne Mission" coming into South America, they volunteered for whatever field might be entered.

We scarcely had purchased Manantiales when John and Bea left El Chaco, Argentina, and started for Colombia, with daughters Sonia and Dorothy.

Not long after the Palmer family arrived in Medellin, John showed that in addition to beautiful Spanish, he had also acquired a perfect technique for driving an automobile in Latin lands. His explanation was, "You've got to scare them before they scare you!" It must be admitted that John usually succeeded in this skill that he had learned so well from other gentlemen of the road. Not infrequently his passengers shared the tremors he managed to communicate to the drivers of others cars. He was an excellent motorist, and in all things John wanted speed and action.

John was a Spirit-filled, no-nonsense Britisher of athletic build, ruddy face, ready hand; and he was content to die for his convictions or to achieve the goals of the mission. His mastery of colloquial Spanish and his practical experience in construction fitted him for taking charge of the seminary building program.

In August 1944, John Palmer and his family moved into the "Big House," as we started calling the original ten-room dwelling at Manantiales, and set up a command post for overseeing the new construction. This was the beginning of the buildings projected in the layout Bill Gillam had drawn, which today house the United Biblical Seminary of Colombia.

Colombia building operations of those days were very different than in England or the United States. Each door and window had to be built in small shops, often one-man establishments, and which usually contracted for them one door or window at a time. None of the carpenters seemed in a financial position to produce the quantity needed. To start even one door or window usually required a deposit to purchase materials. Thereafter, it took repeated small payments and continuous visits to keep the work progressing. One familiar with modern assembly lines can scarcely imagine how torturous was the road to getting delivery on these contracts. But John Palmer had the Spanish, the drive, the experience, and the physical stamina to carry through these time-consuming tasks—and keep on smiling.

In ordering lumber, John had to select the individual pieces, then load them on a horsecart and bring them to the building site. Otherwise, knotty, twisted boards would be brought out instead of select, high grade lumber.

I would not have anyone make villains out of our Colombian friends in the building trades. Their peccadilloes seem slight, compared to wheeler-dealer operations in the United States. More than anything else it was an absorbing and often profitable game which was carried on with endless zest, useful as a means of sharpening one's wits. It added to the evident enjoyment of all but, perhaps, the gringo purchaser; and he didn't matter too much, except as a source of dollars. It would have been rude and unthinkable to accuse anyone of cheating or stealing. What! Just for playing a game! Just because of doing business in the usual way!

In fairness it should be stated that the Antioquians were

superb artisans in cement, plaster, tile, brick, and stone. Men worked just as hard as the bargains they drove, which, if their word was given, they kept. As John wangled his materials, the building rose.

As to specifications, no matter what the blueprint said, the Colombia builders were determined to save you from mistakes and give you what you ought to have and what they knew you really wanted. They would go quite a ways to oblige you, but there are limits beyond which no self-respecting Antioquian mason could be expected to go.

The upper duplex had a view from its front windows that few sites in the world can better: Andean heights, a valley so tropical the grass was always green, so temperate the trees and vegetation grew as though in a well-kept garden—a river, grazing cattle, cathedral spires, and cute little cabins stuck around the mountainsides, furnishing spots of light at night, like candles burning in the darkness. Of course the ladies wanted picture windows down to the floor to take in all of this—from orange trees in the lower front yard to white-robed clouds dancing slow-paced minuets on the distant mountain rim. The construction boss understood all this perfectly, and the brick masons would measure off that big window down to the floor to show how well they knew the wishes of the *dueño* (owner).

The men were a little slow in finishing that part of the house, but one morning a missionary group went up to look around, and the windows were in. Only, they were at the uniform standard height from the floor!

Why?

How could it be?

Had the men not been told?

Did they not understand?

Oh, yes! Yes, a thousand times yes! they all acknowledged genially. But no house in Antioquia had windows like *that!* No Colombian would *ever* buy such a house as that! They had saved us—because we could not know—from the disaster of such a monstrous mistake!

There was no question that the situation required the poised diplomacy of that British gentleman, John Palmer. Not infrequently, in the top right-hand drawer of a merchant's desk, where he made deals and settled accounts, might be seen, as part of his clerical equipment, the butt of a revolver projecting from among the receipt books, as a reminder that he was thoroughly masculine and ready to defend his life, his fortune, and his sacred honor against all comers. It was also a reminder that here in Colombia we were closer than we knew to the nostalgic frontier days of our western United States.

Later, as the upper duplex was nearing completion, the floors did not measure up to specifications. Despite repeated polishing, the tile failed to shine with promised and normal brilliance. John felt that the contract had not been fulfilled. A deadlock in negotiations threatened. The contractor asked to meet with the administration of the mission. The morning came when the contractor sat down in the office with John at his side.

I noticed that the contractor's coat pocket sagged ominously. From my vantage point on the other side of the desk, I caught a glimpse of a revolver butt. I wondered if he usually wore it when going out to call on his customers, or was this a special occasion? It was hardly a "hidden persuader"! John would have died, if need be, in defending the rights of the mission; but the glad moment came when a settlement was agreed upon.

The contractor claimed that time and use would produce the desired brightness in the tile. He was right. Twenty-five years later the tile does have a much warmer glow, and what are twenty-five years! A mere interlude in the life of one of these Antioquian houses built of rock, brick, cement, and tile.

Along the western side of the Manantiales property was a *quebrada* (ravine) through which the mountain stream tumbled over large black rocks. Thunderstorms occasionally brought flash floods that turned the innocent channel of limpid water into a raging torrent. A study of the land revealed that unless the area of the *quebrada* was utilized as a building site, there would not be room for the necessary seminary buildings. But how could we build over the *quebrada* with margins of safety for floodtime?

Were materials available for the job? Was there a Colombian foreman of sufficient integrity as to be entrusted with it? If we miscalculated and the foundations were carried away, the entire mission enterprise could falter, even fail. If we did not build over the *quebrada,* the future development of the campus was threatened. To go forward required daring engineering and also daring faith.

In answer to prayer came Rafael Meneses, an experienced and able Christian foreman. Also huge concrete pipe appeared in the market. So we decided to carry the stream under the entire length of the building.

But our joy in founding the seminary was not shared by all our neighbors. A gracious and lovely lady, later to become a delightful friend of the mission, who lived on an adjoining estate, paid for the erection of a large statue of the Virgin opposite the entrance to the seminary grounds. When complete, the community was delighted. From aged grandparents to young children, they vied with one another in bringing beautiful flowers to place on the two shelves or steps of the high pedestal. Thus the Virgin was always ringed with fresh blossoms, and at night she glowed in electric floodlights.

As the neighbors watched the workmen excavating for the foundations, pouring the concrete, and laying the immense pipe, they realized fully why the Virgin had been placed there and what she was going to do. If the mission was fool enough to put a building in the pathway of a stream that, in time of storm, carried down tons of white churning water and huge boulders, it was a comparatively easy job for the Virgin to destroy the building and bring the evangelical cause to shame and ill-repute. For them, the logic of the situation was irrefutable. Let them build! The gringos' folly would soon be no more! One real storm and the building would be a thing of the past!

The work progressed so rapidly that by early spring of 1945, the entire mission, including the students, moved to Manantiales to begin the second year of studies. The living room of the Big House became the chapel; twenty-six students, teachers, and missionaries were present the first day. Classrooms were set up wherever space permitted. The mission office was in a tiny children's playroom. Work areas were squeezed out here and there while awaiting completion of the administration building; the men's dormitory was a nearby rented house.

While construction went forward, thirty-one people, not counting visitors, were eating in the dining room of the Big House or at tables along the covered walks of the patios. All food was prepared on a four-burner electric stove. One teacher, condemned for a while to breakfast with the students, almost rebelled at the main dish—a large bowl of oatmeal gruel, with milk and sugar securely boiled in to meet Colombian taste! But growing pains are happy pains!

The continued strain of the building program proved too much for John Palmer's strength. With the administration building only half finished, a physician ordered an immediate furlough—John's first in twelve years!

The cable bringing this news reached Mrs. Cowman in Los Angeles on Febraury 2, 1945. Her response was to closet herself alone in fasting and prayer.

At 8:30 P.M. that evening, she felt assured that prayer would be answered.

6

The Story Golden Letters Tell

ON SATURDAY MORNING, February 3, 1945, Mr. Arthur G. Ball arose at his Santa Monica home in Southern California. He was stirred by a momentous decision.

At family prayers, Arthur said to his wife, "Mabel, I have a secret to tell you."

Her answer surprised him, "Arthur, I know what it is. You are going down to South America to help build the new Inter-American seminary at Medellin."

Arthur Ball, a Christian businessman and building contractor, had given away a fortune made in oil. His philosophy was, "I only save what I give away." God had used the tragic death of an only grandchild to turn his thoughts toward South America.

Later that morning, as Mrs. Cowman and Mr. Bud Kilbourne conferred at the mission office in Los Angeles about the crisis in Colombia, and how to fill John Palmer's place, Arthur Ball knocked at the door and was welcomed in. When he offered to go to Colombia as a volunteer builder, ready to pay all his own expenses, he wondered at their silence, until Mrs. Cowman handed him the cable stating that Palmer was leaving. Then he realized that he was part of something that couldn't *happen*—a miracle that only God could do. For Mrs. Cowman, it was just another answer to prayer.

Then, another miracle: with the uncertainties of travel in wartime, God brought Arthur Ball to Manantiales three days before John Palmer left. This made possible a smoother transfer of building responsibilities.

Arthur also brought with him power equipment for making door and window sash, and producing other needed materials. As he was always laughing at himself, and good-natured with everyone, the workmen willingly carried out his "queer" notions. He often said, "I have half the Spanish language; I have the gestures!" Soon, with the enthusiasm of basketball stars, workmen were producing more doors and windows per day than previously in weeks.

I was privileged to help Arthur make business arrangements with the workers. Each room was a separate contract. One day Arthur said to me with a laugh, "B. H., you know too much Spanish. It takes you too long!" So he began a bargaining session with one of the plasterers, using his Spanish gestures. Smiling, laughing, he made motions as though he was plastering the walls with his bare hands, as he said. "*Cuanto?* [How much?]"

The bid was always made on the basis of square yards. The workman, also enjoying the fun, held up three fingers, as he answered, "*Tres pesos.*"

Arthur shook his head good-naturedly, saying, "Mucho! Mucho!" He then held up *one* finger.

The plasterer shook *his* head and held up *two* fingers.

The Californian slowly held up a second finger, then with the other hand, gestured as though cutting it in two.

The Colombian called on his limited English vocabulary, as he said, "OK!"

So the contract was made for one and one-half pesos per square yard, and the American businessman and the Colombian workman laughed together at all the fun they were having.

Built into the very structure of the Bible Seminary of Colombia was the loving gift of Mrs. Cowman enabling the purchase, the devotion of John Palmer who began the building, the concern for youth of Mr. Arthur G. Ball that caused him to finish the building; the labor of fast, hard-working Colombian artisans; and the sacrificial donations of innumerable friends.

With everyone working at top speed, Arthur Ball's crew finished the kitchen and dining room in the new seminary administration building and opened them to the students on March 28; also, the chapel services left the living room of the Big House and went to the new library room.

The following day, March 29, Mrs. Cowman arrived from Los Angeles, California, radiant with delight for all the beauties of the trip, the loveliness of the Medellin valley, and the joy of meeting her South American "fellow missionaries." She was accompanied by her devoted nurse-companion, Lydia Bemmels.

Mrs. Cowman attended our first Easter sunrise service. Believers from the city joined us in the early morning hours, and together we marched to a hill above the seminary grounds singing, "Holy, holy, holy! Lord God Almighty! Early in the morning our song shall rise to Thee." It was a time of rejoicing.

From the heights, out over the valley, sounded the glorious anthem, "He Arose!" Then, with poignancy and power, Bill Gillam sang, "When the Mists Have Rolled Away." In Spanish, the last line of the chorus concludes, "Then we shall rightly understand without the clouds of yesterday." This was praise and prophecy. Dark mists were to envelop Colombia. It would help us in the days ahead to remember that a glorified Christ can roll them all away. Rev. Julio C. Orozco preached on the text, "If Christ be risen."

During the following days, Mrs. Cowman spoke at the seminary chapel services and to missionaries, friends, and students in the afternoon teas in the Big House, where she shared the battles of faith and glorious victories in many lands. She remained for the first Victorious Life Convention in the month of May, for which vice-president Edwin L. Kilbourne came as speaker.

"Manantiales is the most beautiful mission compound in the world!" Mrs. Charles E. Cowman would often say. She delighted in the majesty of surrounding mountains rising to ten-thousand-foot heights, the green symphony of the valley, and, there below us, the red-tiled white-walled medley of Medellin by day, and by night a sea of light, as though reflecting the glittering stars of the tropical sky.

As always, Mrs. Cowman's presence seemed to attract others of like mind and spirit. Mrs. Kathleen Morgan of Pasto, Colombia, was one of these choice ones. Widowed, when her husband died from typhoid fever, she had continued an adventurous life in the saddle, drinking water from the streams (usually thought to be a death warrant), witnessing, teaching, mending broken souls and bodies—a splended example of what the self-sufficiency and faith of sturdy Plymouth Brethren can accomplish. Mrs. Cowman always felt a special kinship with widows, and these two were inseparable spiritual sisters.

On Sunday afternoon, May 6, the closing day of the convention, Mrs. Cowman told of the missionary call of Charles E. Cowman and Ernest A. Kilbourne (Bud Kilbourne's father), and how God used the Oriental Mission which they founded for the salvation of tens of thousands during succeeding decades.

As Mrs. Cowman concluded her address, she called the students to stand at her right hand by the speaker's platform. Then she held up a small burned-out stub of a candle as she said, "My life is like this small candle: most of it has burned out for Christ."

Then she held up a perfect, large white candle, as she continued, "But you students of the Bible Seminary of Colombia are like this candle; you have your life to live, your youth to bring to Jesus Christ our Lord. I call on you today to dedicate your youth, your strength, your life itself—if God should require it—to evangelize Colombia and the lands of the Southern Cross."

Though we did not know that within three years an explosion of political hatred would give the name *"la violencia"* to ten years of Colombian history, each one present made a dedication unto death for the service of Christ.

There was still one glad surprise—a carefully guarded secret—for Mrs. Cowman, made possible by Arthur Ball and those who worked with him—a beautiful, marble plaque set in the wall of the entrance to the seminary administration building, whose golden letters still shine forth their message of love and gratitude:

To
Mrs. Lettie B. Cowman,
world ambassador of Jesus Christ,
who with her "Streams in the Desert"
made possible the Bible Seminary of
Colombia, this building is gratefully
DEDICATED
May 6, 1945

Each morning Mrs. Cowman came to the breakfast table with some fresh and inspiring message from God's Word. One day she said a most amazing thing. "God's Word declares that He will strike through kings in the day of His wrath. What does the word *king* mean? It means the seat of government. Where is the seat of government for the social, political, and religious power that is here opposing the Word of God? It is in Rome. We should pray for God to strike through Rome."

Was she intimating that eternal Rome could change? Did she hope that the supreme pontiff and conservator of the traditions of the mother church would modify what he had sworn to preserve? Did she believe that he could curb the power of bishops and archbishops who ruled this distant field of the church with the absolutism of medieval Spain? Who would dare suggest that in this twentieth century a Reformation could change the hardened attitudes of four hundred years and turn back the decisions of the Council of Trent? One might as well expect the granite ranges of the Andes to melt and disappear like mist under the morning sun. But this was Mrs. Cowman's expectation. After all, it was *only* impossible!

The God of her faith was the God of the impossible. He had said, "All things are possible." She believed it. She might not know why, but He did. Sadly, before the answer came, she had passed over into the realm of the church triumphant. But come it must, and come it did; though this was in the tomorrows—God's tomorrows. Her job was to believe; God's answer would come in His time. As she would often say, "You have to give God time."

One day in Medellin, as we drove past the cathedral reputed to be the largest all-brick building in the world,

Mrs. Cowman turned to Bill Gillam and said, "Some day you will preach in that church."

It was most amazing. Did God indite such a word? When we see the unbelievable things that are taking place in today's Colombia—the spirit of goodwill, understanding, and fellowship with evangelical Christians that the Catholic church now exhibits it is not too much to believe that this also may literally be fulfilled.

On Sunday, May 18, 1945, at 7:30 P.M., Mrs. Cowman took part in a first "Great Commission" service. Rafael Meneses, the man to whose faithfulness and trustworthiness as foreman we owed in great part the sturdy construction of the seminary administration building, was commissioned for the ministry of the Word at Puerto Berrio.

On this occasion, Mrs. Cowman said, "As a result of the work begun forty-five years ago in Japan, over eight hundred churches sprang up in that country. But God has spoken to me that the glory of the latter house shall be greater than the former. I believe we shall see a thousand churches here in the southland."

The last morning of her visit, the missionary women pinned a corsage of multiple orchids to Mrs. Cowman's shoulder; then, the final farewells spoken, Christ's ambassador to the nations was winging her way back to her "little brown house in the West."

But her ministry in Colombia had just begun. She had set hearts aflame. Before many days, some would prove this with a martyr's valor.

Though Mrs. Cowman in her long life had visited many nations, this was her last trip to a foreign land. Here, as everywhere, she had kindled a burning vision in many hearts that, at whatever cost, would be fulfilled in life or in death.

7

"Jesus Came to Our Town"

THE MORNING BEFORE Mrs. Cowman left Medellin to return to the United States, Hermann Mueller, the refugee from Germany, came to her with a Spanish edition of *Streams in the Desert.* On the flyleaf was a note by John Palmer, dedicating the book to his friend, Jesus Zuleta. On the opposite page, Jesus had written, "Mrs. Lettie B. Cowman," and underneath her name had penned:

"The Virgin Mary used to be my spiritual mother, but now through the blessings which I have received from Mrs. Lettie B. Cowman, she is my spiritual mother." Zuleta was so timid and retiring that he had asked Hermann Mueller to secure Mrs. Cowman's autograph.

It may surprise you to know that the name Jesus is a common name in South America, and in Spanish it is pronounced *Hay-soos,* accenting the second syllable.

Jesus Zuleta was a slightly built, intellectual type, somewhat slow of speech, nearsighted, and very dependent upon his glasses. He was first introduced to the mission at a gathering in the home on La Avenida. The businessman who brought him said. "This is Jesus Zuleta, a young friend of mine. He graduated successfully from the Catholic seminary, and has served the church in various capacities. His family, however, are members of the liberal political party. Because he would not recant these political beliefs, the clergy refused to grant him holy orders."

We found him to be a cultured, refined, young man, spiritually hungry for God. Thus began many evenings of communion and fellowship over a period of months. Through the Word of God, he came to know more perfectly the way of salvation.

His physical weakness and lack of funds made him hesitate to apply for study in the seminary; but his desire was discovered, and he was enrolled. His meeting with Mrs. Cowman fired him with a desire to win others for Christ.

One evening, shortly after Mrs. Cowman had returned to the United States, Jesus Zuleta came to the seminary office to say that he and a fellow student felt God was directing them to distribute gospels in the towns of San Pedro and Entrerrios. I warned him of the dangers, for this area was in the higher Andes where traditionalism held sway. He assured me that he and his friend felt they must go despite any danger.

The following Saturday morning at five o'clock, it was my privilege to meet these two students for prayer. Together we read Deuteronomy 2:36 and 31:6: "There was not one city too strong for us; the LORD our God delivered all unto us. Be strong and of a good courage, fear not, nor be afraid of them; for the LORD thy God, he it is who doth go with thee; he will not fail thee, nor forsake thee." After prayer, I drove the young men into the city to catch the early bus.

At ten o'clock Sunday morning, the telephone at Manantiales rang, and an anonymous caller, who called himself an official in the city of Santa Rosa de Osos said, "Your men have been attacked. One has been killed, the other seriously wounded. Come to Santa Rosa de Osos." Then abruptly hung up.

Jesus Zuleta and his companion had gone to an area that was three hours away by horseback from the city of Santa Rosa de Osos. Why was this call coming from that most dangerous city in Colombia? Was it a ruse? What did God want done? The answer seemed clear: "Go!"

Gilberto Vargas, a seminary student, drove the car. He had always wished for permission to travel at faster speeds. That morning, though the road was rough, winding, and dangerous, I urged him to drive at top speed. One stop was made to pick up Dr. Francisco Navarro, a friendly physician and surgeon, a man of widest sympathies. At considerable personal sacrifice he left a large group of patients waiting outside his office. We arrived at Santa Rosa de Osos shortly after noon.

At the entrance to the town, several policemen were waiting. They said that Jesus Zuleta had been wounded and his companion reported killed in the town of Entrerrios. The police had arranged for a plainclothesman to accompany us. Gilberto remained in Santa Rosa to protect the automobile, while Dr. Navarro, the plainclothes' policeman, and I started the three-hour horseback ride to Entrerrios.

After some hours we came to a hill from which we could see the quaint old town of Entrerrios, its red-tile roofs dingy with age, set in a lush green valley through which meandered a peaceful river. Dr. Navarro said, "Let us pray," and led in a simple, sincere word of entreaty.

The plainclothesman then suggested, "Let me ride on ahead, and you come later." He did not wish to be identified with the Evangelicals and to become involved in any disturbance that their presence might cause.

A few minutes later, Dr. Navarro led the way into the town. At the doctor's suggestion, we kept our eyes fixed upon the horses' ears or the pommel of our saddles. Dr. Navarro did not wish us to be stopped for question or argument by the restless groups of men who filled the streets.

Going directly to the hotel where we hoped to find Zuleta, we rode our horses through the wide open hotel doors on the street level, and turned our mounts over to Mariano, a friendly stableboy. After we walked up the rough board steps, the proprietress of the hotel greeted us and pointed to one side of the rather rude lobby where Jesus Zuleta lay on a hard wooden cot.

His clothing was disheveled, his face and head covered with caked mud and blood, and he was as pale and quiet as though dead. But no, the doctor roused him and began dressing his wounds and making a careful record of them. He received the doctor's attentions without response. It seemed as though all life and blood had been drained from him. At the doctor's orders we moved Jesus' cot into a room where he could have more quiet and privacy.

A horse and saddle or a chair strapped to the back of a sturdy mountaineer were the conveyances Zuleta might have used to leave Entrerrios. Next morning it was easy to see that the wan, battered young man could not accept either. He needed days of rest and nourishing food before he could travel. Dr. Navarro had to return to his home and office, but it was my privilege to remain with the wounded man. He could scarcely talk, except to answer questions in monosyllables; but gradually, a phrase here, a sentence there, and comments of visitors gave a picture of what happened.

Jesus and his companion arrived by bus in the town of

San Pedro. There, as they drank a cup of coffee, a man came up and asked, "Where are you going?"

"To Entrerrios," they answered.

The stranger warned them, "If you come to Entrerrios you will be attacked."

The normally timid young man, Jesus Zuleta, replied, "Though they make our body into atoms, we are going." He had a vision of Charles E. Cowman, missionary warrior, and of the Lord when He steadfastly set his face to go to Jerusalem.

After reaching Entrerrios the young men secured a hotel room, and at once went to prayer. Before long, the man who had threatened them in San Pedro made good his words. Standing in front of the large church, which stood imposingly on the high side of the plaza, he began shouting the alarm.

Aroused and urged on by this man, who was head of the city's schools, a thousand men (so the story went) filled the street in front of the hotel. The members of the mob began yelling and shouting threats and attempting to enter, but the hotel doors were locked on the inside. When the mayor of the city came, demanding entrance in the name of the law, the proprietress had to open.

With that, the mayor stepped back, and the mob thundered up the wooden stairway, through the lobby, into the room where the two boys were kneeling. Rough *campesinos* (peasants) threw them across a table and beat them with their fists, then took them to the head of the stairs and literally kicked them down into the hands of the infuriated crowd below.

Here, machete blows began to rain on them with the flat side of the blade, but which still often cut through the flesh; others hurled stones at them. Zuleta's companion managed to escape.

In the meantime Jesus Zuleta's glasses were knocked off and trampled into the ground, but he kept sufficient self-possession to say to those who struck and abused him, "God bless you! God bless you!" As the mob swept him along toward the outskirts of the town, Zuleta was shoved over a low cliff. As he landed on loose dirt at the base, he ran to the river, dove in, came up on the other side, and hurried to hide in the underbrush.

It was late evening as the crowd rushed back through town and crossed over the river on the bridge; then they began searching for him with homemade torches and flashlights.

Before long, as they beat the brush, they discovered him. Again he sought to escape by diving into the river and swimming downstream. A barrage of rocks and sticks fell around him, some striking him. So great was the danger of being stunned and drowning, that he came ashore once more.

Jesus now realized that they intended to kill him. A terrific blow from a machete or rock opened up the back of his head and almost felled him. He dropped to his knees as he prayed Stephen's prayer, "Lord Jesus, do not lay this to their account! And receive my soul!" Then he became unconscious.

When he awakened, all valuables had been taken from his pockets, but one of the men now stood over him with a drawn machete in his hand. This man shouted defiantly at the surrounding mob, "What wrong has this man done since he entered our city? During this whole afternoon, as we have been tormenting him, he has only said, 'God bless you! God bless you!' Now he has invoked the holy name of Jesus. You'll have to kill *me* before you can kill *him!"*

Then another man drew his machete as he too came forward in defense of the fallen youth. The crowd's thirst for blood and violence must have been satiated; at least, they permitted Jesus to pull himself to his feet, swaying with weakness. One of the men let him lean on his shoulder; and so, slowly and painfully, he made his way back to the hotel, where twenty-four hours later, we found him.

During the next three days, as Jesus lay so still and wan upon his cot, an interesting stream of visitors came to see him: well-dressed young ladies, businessmen, all classes. Many of them appeared ashamed and sorry for what had happened. One big *campesino* seemed to speak for the town, as he stood at the foot of the cot. He pushed his big black hat back from his forehead; then, arms akimbo, looking down upon the prone figure, he said, "Jesus came once, and they crucified Him! Now Jesus came to our town, and we did the same. We crucified him!"

As high and low, men and women, came to pay their respects, all admired Jesus' courage and true Christian spirit in the face of death. To each, Jesus gave a word of greeting or a brief phrase of testimony; then I would read for him from the Spanish New Testament.

Even the mayor who had demanded that the hotel doors be opened and thus turned the mob loose upon Jesus also came. What would the young man say to him? Would he upbraid this official for betraying his trust instead of attempting to keep the peace? No, he took the mayor's hands in both of his, as he said most kindly and lovingly, "Thank you for coming, Don Manuel. God bless you! And thank the people of the town for their kindness to me." *Kindness!* It was an astounding word, but I knew he meant it and spoke every syllable in true Christian love.

When Jesus could mount a horse, we began the return trip to Santa Rosa de Osos. We made frequent rest stops at homes en route, where Jesus gave his testimony to the country people who had heard of the riot and seemed to sympathize with him. From Santa Rosa de Osos, we took the bus to Medellin.

In less than a month after Mrs. Cowman's farewell, Jesus Zuleta, one of the mildest of men, had demonstrated spiritual bravery of the highest order: he lived the seventh chapter of Acts—in Colombia.

This was an intimation of mob action, fire, sword, and gunfire that all witnesses for Christ, whether missionaries or nationals, soon would be facing, as mere sporadic violence became the widespread national agony of *la violencia* (the time of violence).

8

Why Some Colombians Think Missionaries Are Naive

WHEN SO MUCH HAPPENS so fast, it almost seems that time stands still; and yet, how strange it is, that when old familiar dates roll around we are shocked to think how brief life is. Joy comes from seeing God do so much despite our frailty, foolishness, and lack of endurance. And so, the muffled sound of distant firecrackers in the Medellin Valley surprised us that another Christmas season was upon us, our first at the Bible Seminary of Colombia.

This year, *globos,* those big fiery balls that floated around the valley, were not only watched, but the missionary children and members of the student body had the fun of making and launching them. In addition to the jollity of making these big, many-colored paper balloons and putting them in the sky, they also tied on gospel cargo—the offer of a free book, a New Testament, to anyone returning them. In this way they got back the balloon for another flight and put another New Testament in circulation. Best of all, they had the oportunity of becoming acquainted with the youth who recovered them.

Probably because of increased and more informal contacts with Colombians, this Christmas season the missionary group was introduced to a new Spanish word—*aguinaldo.* If it is recognized in the Spanish lexicons or used in any other department than Antioquia, we did not have time to discover. When first heard, one might be beguiled into thinking it was another way of saying "Merry Christmas!" But our Colombian friends were careful to fully explain its meaning.

Aguinaldo is really a Christmas game adapted to the Antioquian's acquisitive instinct. When acquaintances meet, whoever says *"aguinaldo"* first (according to the instructions received) must be given a Christmas present by the other. Noblesse oblige almost forbade North Americans turning the tables on poor Colombian students, maids, friends, vendors, and others. It was surprising how swiftly one's shopping list grew under this system. Sometimes we wondered if the word *aguinaldo* had been invented for our special benefit!

Medellin policemen in those days were friendly fellows, and they also picked up this *aguinaldo* custom, adding it to their other amiable traits. They would stop your car as a matter of course—first, to *get* acquainted with you, and afterward because they *were* acquainted with you. The policemen along the three mile road to town knew all our names, our business, how many children we had, and whether anybody at home was ill. And, of course, the missionary knew them by name and most of their vital statistics. As the top speed limit anywhere in the Medellin valley was twenty miles per hour, to be stopped on a trip to town produced little strain on the brakes or one's disposition.

Part of a policeman's duty was to catch traffic violators—particularly speeders. Without aid from radar, bicycle, motorcycle, or automobile, they stood along the highways, a bit out of sight. Any North American driving an automobile anywhere the speed limit is twenty miles per hour might be considered ipso facto a violator. But how gently, how courteously, with what delicate reticence the policeman would flag down a motorist. Briefly, the dialogue would follow this pattern, as the policeman began questioning the offending missionary:

"Buenos dias, Don Eduardo! How are you?"

"Muy bién, gracias, Don Alejandro. How are you? And how is your family?"

"Well, thank you, and may God be thanked too. How is yours?"

Finally, to relieve the policeman's embarrassment, the missionary asks, "By the way, Don Alejandro, might it be that I was exceeding the speed limit just a little?"

"Yes, Don Eduardo. I am very sorry to say you were."

"How fast was I going?"

Invariably the answer was, "You were going sixty kilometers an hour" (about thirty-eight miles—almost twice the speed limit!). No one in his right mind would think of disputing it.

You mention apologetically and obliquely the incoming plane you were to meet, or whatever was weighing upon your mind.

"I know! I know, Don Eduardo. You will do better another time. And pardon me for taking your time!"

Oh, such blessed, friendly, understanding policemen. You wonder, why can't all policemen everywhere be like that? And—as you drive away—you almost forget the twenty mile per hour speed limit!

When this first Christmastime at Manantiales approached, policemen stopped missionary cars as a matter of course, but now they called out "Aguinaldo!" It was almost unthinkable that a missionary would turn the tables on a policeman any more than he would on a student.

But one day the worm turned. To a Colombian student I was the first to shout, "Aguinaldo!" Now I had him, or did I? This young man was an Antioquian, and Antioquians are the shrewdest traders in South America.

Without the slightest embarrassment or hesitation, the student put an arm over my shoulder, and with his other hand pointed to a distant mountain, as he said, "Don Benjamin, do you see that beautiful mountain? Well, I give it all to you; its timber, its gold and emeralds, its undiscovered mines, its lovely fountains and rivers."

Aha! Now I knew how one handles this "aguinaldo" situation! No wonder Colombians sometimes think missionaries are naive!

And all the while, by *globos* overhead, by gospels and tracts that students took with them back into their homes in town or village, in programs for groups of believers who were beginning to meet in homes, the "good tidings of great joy" was announced: "Unto you is born this day in the city of David a Saviour, which is Christ the Lord."

But forces, seemingly beyond anyone's control, were moving Colombia toward such an ordeal as missionaries had never dreamed of and would never forget, and which, for some, would make the decision to return after their first furlough a dedication deeper than they had ever previously known.

9

Puñaletas!

The Inter-American Mission gave Burton and Bernadine Biddulph and their children, Howard and Judy, a joyous welcome when they arrived in Medellin July 28, 1946.

Burton had left a chaplaincy with a captain's rating in the United States Army. He had served with the troops that took Remagen Bridge in the Battle of the Bulge. He had been on active duty there the night when the life expectancy of military police who directed traffic was only twelve minutes. His outfit served for a time under the command of the famous tank commander Gen. George Patton. Later, at Manantiales, I asked Burton if his life had been in as great danger in Colombia as on the field of battle in World War II. He replied, "A number of times I have been closer to death in Colombia than I ever was in Europe during World War II." Let's take a look at the anatomy of one such experience.

As with all missionaries, language school was the primary responsibility of Burton and Bernardine during the first year. John Palmer had so filled missionaries and language school students with a vision of aggressive evangelism that on their own, they planned a gospel distribution campaign in the nearby town of Envigado. This was to be a prelude to opening a mission hall in that locality. Burton and Bill Gillam were leaders of the group. The forty-two persons taking part left from the language school in a large bus and a jeep. Burton later described to us his first "action" in Colombia.

The plan apparently worked successfully. All crusaders reached their assigned post in Envigado. After distributing gospels throughout the town on schedule, all of them but Gene Wittig and Jose Ruiz, a boy from Chiquinquira, made their way successfully to the image of the Virgin where the bus and the jeep which had brought out teams was waiting. The rest remained there, determined to keep faith with the two missing members of the group, hoping each instant they would appear.

As the townspeople began to gather, the missionaries saw that there might be trouble, and suggested to the bus driver that he take them a little farther out of town, where they could await the arrival of Gene and Jose.

The chauffeur drove the bus perhaps a quarter of a mile farther out to a wide place in the road where there were piles of road-building rock. Almost at the same moment Bob Crosby of the Wesleyan Mission drove up and parked his jeep behind the bus. Then the violence started.

A moment later a truck came roaring out of Envigado filled with men yelling, "Long live the Virgin! Long live the Catholic church! Down with the Protestants!" This truck drove directly in front of the bus, thus blocking any chance of a getaway.

About half of the missionary party were men. They jumped down from the school bus and tried to face these shouting, cursing men who already were picking up rocks from the abundant supply at the side of the road and hurling them at the bus. As the missionaries ran toward the Colombian men, they sought to corner them one by one to make a personal contact with them. They stood there with rocks in their hands yelling, "You don't believe in the Virgin!"

The missionaries had given away all their gospels, so Burton shouted to the man in front of him, "Give me a gospel! Give me one! Let me show you what it says!"

As Burton continued begging for a gospel, one man dug into his pocket and defiantly held one out.

Burton turned at once to the words of Elizabeth addressed to Mary, "Blessed art thou among women, and blessed is the fruit of thy womb. And why is this granted to me, that the mother of my Lord should come to me?"

Then this new missionary continued with the words of Mary, "My soul doth magnify the Lord, And my spirit hath rejoiced in God my Saviour."

Gradually the men quieted down and finally got back into their truck and drove away. With this, the language school bus started for Medellin. But as Gene Wittig and Jose were still unaccounted for, Bob Crosby, Dr. Roberts (a medical missionary of HCJB radio station), Bill Gillam, and Burton felt that they should wait and take them out in the jeep.

After two or three minutes they realized that they had done the wrong thing. Though not yet very long in Colombia, they had begun to understand that when a mob gets two or three men cornered, they will do away with them, even when they wouldn't attack a larger group. The missionaries knew that they had to get out of there soon if they were to get out alive. So they started with the jeep toward Medellin.

Sure enough, when they reached a turn in the road, they saw that the mob which had surrounded them a few minutes before had let the language school bus go through, but they had parked their truck across the narrow road—

the only place where the jeep could have turned off for Medellin, and to make sure, they had strewn the road with rocks.

As the four men pulled up and stopped, these fellows began the same yelling and shouting as before. Bill and Burton got out and tried to outyell the crowd in attempt to get their attention. They wanted to develop some kind of dialogue with the townsmen, or at least put off what they thought was sure death.

But neither Bill nor Burton could make himself heard. They shouted, "Well, kill us if you want to, but tell us why! What's the trouble? Why are you after us?" They wanted to get the men to talk back, to create some kind of rapport with them. The missionaries couldn't even get their attention; the mob was infuriated. So they went around to the driver's side of the truck, and there they could see the nationals pulling tools out from under the seat. They figured this was their doom.

Then they all looked up, and here came a bus out of Envigado, pell-mell down the road. The first truck was already across the road in front of the jeep; now this second bus came skidding to a stop behind it. The missionaries were hemmed in on all sides. About forty men poured out of this other bus; and with those from the first truck, this made about eighty men.

When this second bus came to a stop, a priest also jumped out into the middle of the group. The men who had come with him were pulling knives from under their shirts. These three-cornered knives are called *puñaletas.* They are made from three-cornered saw files. These *puñaletas,* made from the finest file steel, are ground down to a point like a needle, and the three sides are honed to a razor edge. They draw no blood, for the skin closes right over the wound. They are deadly. Criminals carry them, and assassins use them for exterminating their victims. The men who had no knives ran to pick up rocks.

Later, one wonders why he does certain things. He doesn't know why at the moment. But inspired by the Lord, or acting intuitively, the missionaries walked right toward the priest, who was in the middle of the crowd; they were determined to try to save their lives if they could. They talked to the priest, trying to get him to quiet the mob.

Burton later remembered distinctly the sensation that they were going to get stabbed in the back while they were talking to the priest. He said he could practically feel those needle-sharp *puñaletas* going through his back!

The priest was red in the face and shaking all over. He might have thought that he was going to find Colombians instead of Americans, but all four of these men were missionaries. And every one of them knew that they were near what seemed certain death.

Burton didn't see what happened; but as he was talking to the priest, something hit him on the side of the head, scraping the skin off one side of his face, and plowing grooves through the flesh.

However, the priest must have given orders, for the truck that blocked the road ahead of them began to get out of the way.

As they had gone around the hood of the bus to talk with the priest, they were a bit protected. But as soon as they turned and started for the jeep, the men cut loose with those rocks. A large one struck Bill in the back, practically disabling him.

When the truck started pulling away from in front of them, the four jumped into the jeep. But there was no cover; the rocks kept coming.

When Bob Crosby put the jeep in gear, they discovered that the four tires were flat. Up till now the fellows with the *puñaletas* had used them on the tires, not on the missionaries!

They barely crept away with those flat tires. A curve in the road put the four out of sight, and they turned in to the Country Club, hid the jeep, and phoned the police. The officers came and took them into Medellin, where they took a taxi to Manantiales.

Gene Wittig and Jose Ruíz showed up later. They had been attacked and kicked, then picked up by the police who got them out of town on the police van.

The next day, Bill and Burton were still so shaken by the experience, so bruised and aching from the stoning, that others insisted on filling their Sunday preaching appointments in Puerto Berrio. Bill recovered only slowly from the injury to his back. For several years he suffered recurrences of pain and lameness.

Later that same afternoon a seminary student went out to Envigado on his own to assess results and determine the attitudes of the people. He found a group of leading businessmen in a café discussing the riot with city officials. They were all mystified as to what had caused the violence. That interest in the gospels was deep and that people who had them were hanging on to them was shown when one of the men said, "I will pay two pesos to anybody to get me one of those little books!"

Sometimes wildest storms prepare earth for richest harvests.

10

"This Is War!"

On Friday, December 15, 1947, Burton and Bernardine Biddulph, accompanied by Prof. Henry Parra and a seminary student, arrived in Barbosa, department of Santander. Gilberto Vargas, seminary student-pastor, welcomed them.

One month before this, Burton had been in Barbosa to baptize ten converts. Now Burton was back to baptize fifteen others on the following Sunday and to receive them as members of the church.

One of the candidates for baptism lived fifty miles from Barbosa. To visit him meant a round trip by jeep through a part of Colombia where men had begun to play politics "for keeps," but Burton felt they should do all possible to see that the young man did not miss the service.

Moniquirá, a nearby city, would later be singled out by one historian as the place where the savage period of political violence in Colombia, known as *la violencia,* began in 1948. In this region, even now, Colombians were killing Colombians, and Catholics were killing Catholics because of fierce political loyalties that had been building toward this climax since the founding of the Republic. The previous day four people had been shot to death for political reasons on the road over which Burton and his companions planned to travel.

The young man whom they purposed to visit, Jose Ruíz,

had formerly attended institute classes at the seminary in Medellin. When Jose returned to his home from the Bible institute, he took with him a box of gospels. He wanted to bring to his friends and neighbors the transforming truth which he had received. The distribution of these gospels had aroused opposition, and the local religious leader had ordered the police to find and burn them.

The young man's father, though a faithful practicing Catholic and sufficiently acceptable politically as to have been named municipal judge, resented having a member of his family treated so shabbily. Due to the activist zeal that was infecting everyone, in addition to wearing his machete, he strapped on a revolver and a belt of ammunition, and informed the misguided minions of the law that the first man he saw set fire to one of his son's gospels would be killed on the spot. Enthusiasm for burning gospels waned notably.

The rough rock-ballasted road that Burton and his party followed wound through the city of Saboyá, Henry Parra's hometown. Because of this, the trip was doubly dangerous for Professor Parra. He had formerly served as superintendent of public education in this town, and was living there at the time of his conversion. They hated him for having apostatized to the Protestants; and in the political passions that now swept over Colombia, his life, as a liberal, was forfeit in a conservative town such as Saboyá. But, to a man whose point of honor is well developed, danger may be an irresistible attraction, perhaps only to prove to himself that he is not afraid.

As the mission jeep drove through the town of Saboya no one was on the streets nor in the public square except two policemen and a man who, in the past, was named to kill Parra.

A few miles farther on, Burton and Bernardine stopped to visit a famous shrine, while Henry Parra continued with the student pastor and a local boy to guide them to Jose's home.

When the young man's father, the municipial judge, greeted the three visitors, he cordially invited them to inspect a homemade sugar mill on his small farm.

Soon a truck filled with armed men drove up in front of the farmer's house. A man called out from the truck, "The chief of police has come at your call."

Jose's father heard the yells and excused himself to see what was happening. To the statement that he had called for the police chief, he replied, "That is not true. I called for no one."

The police chief shouted, "But the Protestants have come to take your son, and we have come to defend you and him."

Jose's father answered, "But our constitution grants religious liberty in Colombia."

"Constitution! What is that?" replied the angry chief. "There is no constitution here, except that this is a Catholic town, and we are here to kill any Protestants who come."

"These Protestants are under my roof," Jose's father informed them. "They are now part of my family." His revolver and machete added weight to his words.

"But they are kidnapping your son."

"My son is going to their seminary with my consent."

Their angry shouts filled the air as the truck started away; and the armed men yelled meaningfully, "We will be back! We will be back!"

Soon Jose took leave of his father, and the jeep began the return trip to Barbosa.

It was growing dark when the jeep picked up Burton

and Bernardine Biddulph at the shrine. As they passed through Saboyá, the town where Henry Parra formerly resided, doors were sealed, most windows boarded up, and scarcely a light was to be seen. An ominous stillness pervaded the darkened and deserted streets.

A few miles beyond Saboyá they came to Garavito. As the travelers crossed over the railroad line that sliced through the town, the lights of the jeep shone against a white building on the far side of the tracks, where the travelers could see men running to hide behind a pile of railroad ties by which they must pass. These men turned their flashlights upon the speeding jeep. Almost certain of a shower of bullets, the group huddled together in the jeep; but nothing happened.

Looking back toward Garavito, they could see the group of men following them, turning a flashlight in their direction occasionally. It was strange. Were these deliberate killers who knew that the men they were after could not escape?

A quarter of a mile after passing the group at the railroad crossing, the lights of the jeep flashed into bold relief a rock barricade that had been placed across the narrow road since they passed in the afternoon. It extended from one bank to the other where a cut through high ground made a detour impossible. The roadblock of large boulders was heaped high in the center.

As Henry Parra stepped on the brakes, stopping short, he shouted, "I can't get out! I'm ambushed! There isn't a chance! Don't one of you get out! There are armed men on the bank!"

Burton Biddulph, who had served with the fighting men of the First Army's divisions as they slashed their way into

Germany on "The Road of the Purple Heart," said, with solemn emphasis, "This is war!"

Burton not only knew war, he knew jeeps. He had driven them in the military columns that pushed day and night across Germany toward the costly victory of World War II. In a land so torn by hatred as Colombia, he knew death was imminent. Burton, with the instinct of an army man who has driven his jeep weary miles over battlefields, reached down, shifted the four-wheel drive gears into mesh, as he yelled into Henry's ear, "Give it the gun!"

Bernardine, eyes staring fearfully at the boulders ahead, cried out, "Burton, you can't do it. This jeep can't get over!"

Henry Parra knew that Burton's actions and his words were equivalent to the command, "Go through at any cost! Give it all you've got! There's no other escape!" He knew also that Burton was demanding a miracle.

The jeep was now in compound low gear. The jeep's engine roared. The passengers shook and bounced as the wheels ground into the rocks, groaning, heaving, lifting. High in the air, the axles, engine, transmission, and floor were crashing against the rocks. As they hung there balancing on the barricade, the four wheels still turned.

Were they to be left teetering on the high center? Was there no traction? Was this the end? But, then, a wheel caught on a rock, the jeeped lurched crazily—then another, another! They were moving a bit forward—yes, forward—half an inch, an inch—wheels turning, catching a stone here and there; they moved a wee bit ahead—jumping, leaping, jerking ahead. Then, with a terrible jolt the wheels hit the roadbed on the other side of the barricade. Their heads jerked back from the sudden speed, as four wheels gripped the road. Unbelievably, the barrier was behind them, they were speeding toward friends, loved ones, safety—their life a gift from God for further service for the Lord!

As they raced on into the darkness, the only sounds were the roar of the engine, the grinding of the gears, the thump of the tires over the road. You don't talk when you've been near death. At last Bernardine broke the silence. She said, defensively, "Well, I've got my *cédula* [Colombian residence permit]!"

That they did not laugh at this assertion of her rights to travel Colombia's roads is a measure of how well they realized that they had had a close brush with death. Henry Parra simply said, "These people don't read!"

Later, retelling the experience, Henry said, "I know trucks. I have driven them. There is no truck ever made that could have driven over that roadblock. As for an automobile, that is altogether impossible."

It may have been impossible for a jeep. But not that night!

Sunday, December 17, 1947, under the brilliant Colombian sun, where the white waters of the Suarez River poured over a huge granite boulder into a large pool, Burton Biddulph baptized fifteen, splendid Colombian young people.

On the riverbanks stood the witnesses: Gilberto Vargas; his sister Ines, a schoolteacher; the children of the school; the membership of the church; and a company of townspeople. For Burton this meant twenty-five baptisms in one month. For these youth it meant twenty-five decisions to serve Christ faithfully unto death.

As a chaplain at the Remagen Bridge in Germany and as a missionary on the rocky road of the department of Santander, Burton had discovered that a man whom God has chosen is indeed immortal till his work is done.

11

"A la Grande!"

As John Palmer returned from his furlough, once again he fanned the flame of devotion to gospel distribution and quickened the mission and churches with a vision for this crusade ministry. Under his leadership the students of the seminary vied with one another in going ever farther afield. Each town or city visited revealed others beyond. Because of its history, its importance, and the possibility of violent reaction, it was inevitable that the crusades would reach Segovia.

The town of Segovia in the northern part of the department of Antioquia continued a tradition of gold mining with a history not only embracing the colonial and modern periods but also the Indian empires of the past. A visit to the House of Gold in the Bank of the Republic in the capital city of Bogotá would reveal a glittering and amazing display of gold dishes, gold bracelets, gold necklaces, gold nose rings, gold earrings, gold figurines, gold gods and goddesses—rooms filled with golden objects wrought into every kind of serviceable vessel and decorative ornament, all dating from the Indian period prior to Europe's discovery of the Americas.

The Indians' love for gold was one reason for today's scarcity of Indian people in Antioquia. The Spanish conquistadores who came here plucked earrings and nose rings from the quivering flesh and lopped off heads, making it easier to secure the precious metal which the Indians had mined and wrought so artistically into neckbands. While the Indians disappeared from Antioquia, the lust for gold remained in those who took their place. Gold fever, as in the town of Segovia, usually expressed itself in drinking, gambling, carousing, and the "quick draw" typical of our own early West. Little wonder that the gospel had not reached here yet.

When John Palmer presented Segovia as a crusade objective, the students responded with weeks of prayer at the daily six-thirty A.M. meeting in the seminary chapel. The excitement which preceded tackling this legendary area resulted in many volunteers.

The Colombians felt at first that it was best for only Colombians to go; the presence of American missionaries might increase the people's resentment. John Palmer selected Julio Orozco and student-teacher Henry Parra as the first team to enter Segovia. The two men were delighted with their appointment.

On their first weekend visit to Segovia, the two men waited until Sunday morning when large numbers were in attendance at the early mass, before beginning distribution. As they walked about town, with the perspiration running down their faces, they quickly placed four hundred ninety-eight gospels in as many hands. With only two hundred thirty-two gospels and two hundred tracts left, they decided to wait until after the mass when more folk would be crowding the market square.

As the people poured forth from the church, Henry was soon lost in the crowd that surged around him and found himself without tracts or gospels; for the people, either curious or anxious for the Word, had taken them all. He immediately began to sell Bibles.

Later, Henry learned that Julio, in distributing gospels, had passed in front of the labor union hall where representatives of the one thousand two hundred miners were in session. Some of the men rushed him into the building, where he disposed of all his tracts and gospels. When the two crusaders met again, they were without literature. As they remembered some New Testaments left in the hotel room, they brought these to the market square where they were sold.

Now Henry and Julio could see men everywhere reading the Word. Some stood in groups, listening to another reading; others concealed a gospel or a New Testament in a newspaper to keep it hidden as they read it. Seldom, if ever, had anything like this been seen in the department of Antioquia.

Such was the almost unbelievable entrance of the gospel among the fifty thousand people of this city.

The next week Henry and Julio left for Segovia with thirteen hundred gospels and a supply of Bibles, New Testaments, and tracts—one hundred seventy pounds in all. They spent Saturday night in a Segovia hotel. The next morning while those interested in traditional religion were occupied with their devotions, the two men went out and started down the street that winds along the backbone of the ridge on which a large part of the town extends. Every home was ready to receive a gospel and a tract.

Upon the third visit to Segovia, on a concrete terrace in front of the Catholic church, the two men found a pile of burned fragments. The report was that it consisted of gospels the priest had collected from the people. They must not have been able to secure many gospels, for a large part of the charred remains, upon examination, was found to consist of partially burned motion picture and popular magazines.

The following week, Julio Orozco and Henry Parra faced a real threat. The two representatives of traditional religion in Segovia had brought in a Spanish priest, a noted orator, for a week's mission in their church. They also had built a platform in the plaza to serve as a pulpit for addressing the Sunday crowd.

As the service in the plaza began, Henry and Julio went to their room for prayer. They sensed the aroused traditionalist sentiments of many of the townspeople. The Spanish orator knew how to play upon the sensibilities of his audience. Now and then phrases spoken with unusual emphasis reached them in the hotel, followed by shouted "vivas!" The crusaders knew that only one road led out of town and no plane left until Monday morning. Prudence and their honor forbade them attempting to slip away unseen. This would have forfeited the goodwill of sympathizers and could have caused many to spurn and ridicule them and their gospel.

As the oration and the shouts of the people grew more heated, Henry said to Julio, "We can't sit here in this room and wait for them to come and drag us out. That would be cowardly. Let's go out there and take it for God *a la grande* [in a big way]!" With a spirit that Latin blood makes easier, they left their room, walked to the square, and stood in a conspicuous place on the sidewalk surrounding the plaza.

When the Spanish orator caught sight of them, it set his eloquence aflame. To think that they would flout his presence and defy the authority of the church, sent him into a rage. He pointed at them as those who dared trespass upon the faith of this people; he invoked the image of that other Segovia in Spain that had proven its fidelity to their religion by *autos-de-fe* (the burning of heretics). The shouting increased. Large sections of the crowd approved the sentiments and cried for action. How God would deliver them was not their responsibility; Henry and Julio were determined to take it "in a big way" for God.

As Henry and Julio stood on the plaza sidewalk in defiance of the orator of the day, a gradual movement of men mystified them. One, two, or three at a time the men gathered about them. Before long the two crusaders were surrounded by hundreds of husky, determined-looking fellows. When the Spanish orator completed his peroration, if he expected an attack, it did not occur. Instead, members of the miners' labor union who had crowded around Parra and Orozco to protect them, now congratulated them for having so boldly defied the Spaniard.

To climax this moment, the proprietor of a joint café and saloon came up behind Orozco and Parra and tapped them on the shoulder, as he said, "Do you know who that man is that just tried to get these people to burn you in the plaza? Why, he's nothing but a common drunk. The first thing he ordered sent to his room after he arrived here was a case of whiskey!"

The following Tuesday morning when Henry and Julio reported their adventure to the seminary students, everybody wanted to go to Segovia.

Because of rising resistance by organized religion, even though offset by the support of the powerful labor union, John Palmer felt a permanent work could, and should, be established in Segovia.

12

"There's Been a Murder in Every House!"

THE BRABONS ARRIVED in Colombia the same week as Burton and Bernardine Biddulph. Harold Brabon, a chemist, had worked for and been a personal friend of the older Henry Ford. His wife, Margaret, a speech major and a brunette, all smiles and vivacity, found that the Colombians wanted to claim her as their own. David Brabon, a "native" Colombian through being born in Medellin, had already become a smiling, cooing three-month-old. With language school behind them, the Brabons thought it wonderful good fortune to be chosen as missionaries to Segovia.

According to the scale that Latins use in classifying others, Harold Brabon had that rare quality in an American—*el don de gente* (the gift of people). It is somewhat like charisma or *simpático*—charm—only more so! Beyond simpatico, the quality of *don de gente* declares that you capture instantly goodwill and friendship. It is the total opposite of being an "ugly American." Wherever Harold went, he made friends with persons high and low. As "Harold" is difficult to pronounce in Spanish, he went under the latinized form of his other given name, Arthur, or "Arturo."

When Arturo went to visit Segovia, he found that houses were very scarce. He finally located a two-story dwelling adjacent to an old grocery store which could serve as a chapel.

As Harold stood in front of the place looking things over, Sylvestra, a shoemaker across the street, came to inquire about the newcomer who had appeared in town. He showed great surprise when Arturo told him, "I'm coming to live here, and will be bringing my wife and three-month-old baby."

The wrinkles about the shoemaker's eyes grew a little tighter as he glanced around apprehensively, then, looking up and down the solid rows of doors and windows set in the yellowing white walls, he telescoped the town's history into one sentence: "In the last ten years, there's been a murder in every house along this street!"

Even the personnel of the British-owned Frontino Gold Mining Company, which had operated in Segovia for decades, protested when Harold ("Arturo") Brabon reported what he planned to do. The manager said, "You aren't going to bring your wife and three-month-old baby into *this* town, are you? Why, there is such violence that not even *we* dare go into town on weekends. It's such a violent place that Colombians from other parts won't come here!"

Some reactions on the seminary campus in Medellin also revealed a bit of hesitation. When their appointment was announced, my wife, Emma, said, "Margaret, I am not going to let you and David go with Harold unless God gives me a promise."

Margaret, in recounting this move to Segovia, said, "I remember the day Aunt Emma shut herself into her room for two or three hours. When she came out, she said, 'All right, Margaret, you can go. God has given me a promise.'

"After she read it to me, I underlined it in my Bible and wrote beside it '*Tia* [Aunt] Emma,' and the date. I realized it was a terrific promise; and as we went into Segovia, I thought much about it, but later I forgot it. It is amazing how literally God fulfills His Scriptures."

The first day the Barbons got there, Julio, the Colombian pastor, came and said to Margaret, "I don't think you had better go out into the town. We'll send you a dinner, Doña Margarita."

So the two men went out and left Margaret holding David on her lap. They returned and left with her two *porta-comidas,* those tin stacked-up food carriers. She opened the top one and saw some thick, greasy soup. She wasn't *that* hungry! She went down to the second layer, and there staring back at her were some fish eyes. She was fast losing her appetite. Then she arrived at the third layer—some rice and eggs; but just then a huge rat came into the room. You can guess who got the rice and eggs!

Later, Harold came back, and they started cleaning the place, one room at a time. Harold did not get very far with the cleaning, for every few minutes another man would come in to buy a Bible or talk with him.

Harold, when he related this experience to me, commented, "The whole town was rooting for me because I had the nerve and the confidence in them to bring a pretty girl like Margaret into town. They felt a sense of civic pride to think that I was coming to live there with my wife and baby son."

In some ways living next door to the hall where the meetings were held was very handy for Margaret. From their sleeping room up on the second floor, she could look through cracks in the wall and watch and listen to the services. These usually crowded out the hall with two or three hundred attending—all men. No women came at first.

"When Florence Cavender came over with her accordion," Margaret later recalled, "we announced hymns and started to sing, but I had to laugh. There wasn't anybody in all that crowd except Harold, Florence, and me who knew the words or music! But they liked it, and soon they learned to sing. Later, Bill Gillam came over, and then you should have seen them. They shook their heads and marveled. They had never heard anything like Bill's accordion music and his singing."

It wasn't long before Harold and Margaret learned that the best missionary and personal worker in Segovia was David, their baby boy. He didn't have to speak. He would just smile at men or women, young or old, hold out his pink, chubby hands, snuggle up to them as they took him, and he had won another heart.

The fact that the leaders of traditional religion in Segovia had lost the goodwill of the city, greatly favored the work of the Evangelicals. Nevertheless, two priests who were brothers had a hard core of devotees upon whom they could count.

All the while, Harold made friends with the mayor and the city authorities, as well as with the garbage collector; the workmen in the gravel pit; and Gabriel, the saloonkeeper on the corner. He not only had tracts and gospels, but he enjoyed giving a mango or an orange to the youngsters.

The Frontino Mining Company, a British firm, continued what it had been for decades past—the sustaining industry of the city. The miners not only profited from employment, but also had their own private ways of adding to their daily wages by using all the arts that miners have ever known for getting into their own pockets the gold extracted from company mines. The bolder *machuqueros*—men who slept in the day time and went out at night to be lowered by their accomplices into the airshafts and ventilating holes —surreptitiously dug out the gleaming metal that should have gone to the British owners but instead fed the fever that was theirs.

Margaret had never been able to understand the large supplies of expensive canned goods on store shelves. The prices were so ridiculously high that she couldn't think of buying them. Who could?

One day she saw a little old wrinkled lady dressed in rags come into a store and buy a can of beans at a tremendous price. She could not figure it out. What did it mean?

Ruth Connel, wife of an administrator of the mines told Margaret, "Oh, that woman is the wife of a *machuquero*— one of those men who steal gold from the mines during the night. She will take that can of beans and let it down an air vent to her husband. Sometimes as many as two hundred *machuqueros* work the mines at night. Most of them previously worked for the company. They know where the vein of gold runs, and they just stay down there and hide by day."

Ruth Connel's husband spoke up, "Yes, I've been down there and found them. But I didn't question them. My life would have been worth nothing. I just walked on."

The *machuqueros* endangered the Frontino Mining operation by weakening the supporting columns of rock left to hold up the forty subterranean levels, through digging gold out of them where they pleased. So the ancient drama of gold continued still in Segovia.

A man in charge of the big English gold mining firm quipped that the best families in town and some of the largest stores were founded as a result of daring operations of *machuqueros* who graduated into solid and respected citizens!

Knowing what the people in Segovia were capable of, the Brabons were not surprised when peace came to an abrupt halt on the night of November 22, 1947. Two busloads came in from the town of Remedios. Harold and Margaret saw them and thought it was just another fiesta, until two policemen appeared at their door. And across the street an armed guard from the mining company was also marching back and forth. Harold went out and asked them what was the matter. They said, "We are here for your protection." Harold knew that something was up.

Harold told Margaret to put David between the two French doors. That may sound ritzy, but there wasn't anything ritzy about *those* French doors!

Then he said, "You'd better be ready to take to the roofs!" So they went to look at the roof to see where that would take them, and Margaret was ready to "take to" them, because there was only the front door entrance to the whole building.

The Brabons had been warned about all the possibilities. They had read in *La Defensa* newspaper, "By blood or fire we will drive the Protestants out of Segovia!" And now they heard the mob coming up the street crying. *"Viva la Virgen!* [Long live the Virgin!] *Abajo los Protestantes!* [Down with the Protestants!] *Que mueran los herejes!* [Kill the heretics!]" As they came near the house they were working up a mob feeling as only Latins can.

Then, suddenly, a tropical storm burst on the scene. Thunder clapped, lightning flashed, and the heavens opened. The Brabons never saw such a storm before or after that night. The mob was drenched—deluged—with the cloud bursts. They ran to the four ends of the town to find shelter.

Three days later, Margaret said to Harold, "Honey, look how literally God fulfills His promise," and she read to him the promise Aunt Emma had given to her: "He will keep the feet of his saints, and the wicked shall be silent in darkness; for by strength shall no man prevail. The adversaries of the LORD shall be broken to pieces; out of heaven shall he thunder upon them" (1 Sa 2:9-10).

And he poured a flood of rain on them also. Just in time—exactly in time. That Scripture came so alive to the Brabons that they could stand anything after that, knowing whose side they were on. It was also wonderful to them how that promise was given to them beforehand.

The next day Harold went out to the headquarters of the British gold mining company. The administrator asked him if he knew what had happened the night before. Harold thought he did, but there was quite a chapter of which he knew nothing. The manager of the mine said, "You know, the priest came out last night with all his group while we Britishers were having a fiesta in honor of our princess Elizabeth who was being married yesterday.

"He stood out in front and began shouting, 'You have been robbing this country for fifty years. You've been taking our gold. And now you have brought those hated Protestants into Segovia.'

"Now you know as well as we do, Arthur, that we had nothing whatever to do with your coming here."

That, of course, was true; but the church had now started a battle with the mining company. The result was that before long, the avaricious priest and his brother were moved out of Segovia.

Brabons' baby, David, grew and continued to increase

in favor. He was one missionary who would never have to wait for a visa to enter Colombia; native sons are always welcome. Spanish, real Antioquian Spanish, was his native tongue. The first words that Harold taught him to say were, *"Soy Antioqueño* [I am an Antioquian]." It was always a knockdown performance; it put him in command wherever he went.

David's first public appearance was in a program before an audience that overflowed the mission hall. For once, he was paralyzed with stage fright, and he stood frozen. He opened his mouth to quote his scripture verse, "I am the bread of life." But nothing came out. At last, to break the silence, he shouted at the top of his voice, "I'm an Antioquian."

The crowd went wild. It was difficult to restore order. There could be no question about it: David had inherited his father's *don de gente.*

13

"I'm Glad I Didn't Miss It!"

IN THE UNITED STATES, Carol Harding, a youthful, dainty girl had been a public school teacher for nineteen years. Teaching was her career; she loved it. At an early age she had graduated from a teachers college; and when she went to the 1944 OMS missionary convention at Winona Lake, Indiana, she carried with her a signed contract for the following schoolyear. In the one service that she attended, as she sat listening to Mrs. Cowman's address, a most remarkable thing occurred: she *heard* God speak to her. As clearly as though in an audible voice, He said, "Carol, I am calling you to be a missionary!"

Telling it afterward, she said, "What! *Me?* Carol Harding a *missionary!* I was much too old. I had no training for *that!*"

But the voice amazed her, upset her, shook her very soul. What could it mean? She attended no more services of the convention; but so deep was the impression, so powerful the effect of this one message upon her life, that even after the summer ended and she had returned to the classroom again, she kept saying to herself, "Carol Harding, this is your last year teaching in the public school!" She knew God had something else for her; just what, He would have to reveal.

For the time being, she could not think her way past

some such missionary task as teaching in an elementary Christian day school in the United States. To better prepare for this, she went to Los Angeles the following year to take refresher courses in education and to study child evangelism at Biola College.

This brought her in contact with her longtime friend La Verne Ball, and her parents, Arthur and Mable Ball. Earlier in the year Arthur and Mable had gone to Colombia for construction work on the seminary. There they saw large numbers of Colombian children without a chance for schooling. They pleaded with Carol to go to Colombia and start schools for these neglected children. What an astonishing suggestion! Never had it occurred to Carol that God intended *her* to be a *foreign* missionary!

Before long God spoke again. He sent a beloved cousin to visit her. Carol and her cousin were invited to dinner at the Balls' home. There Arthur and Mable again presented the tremendous need of Christian schools for Colombian children.

Later that evening Carol's cousin said, "Carol, if you want to go, I've got a thousand dollars to get you started." How unbelievable!

In a meeting with Carol, Mrs. Cowman—that great champion of faith—said, "Carol, you're not a bit too old. God has just been preparing you to help those dear Colombian children."

Then Bud Kilbourne, who was carrying executive responsibilities, assured her, "Carol, you have enough money to start; and the mission will give you a place to live."

That settled it.

She arrived in Medellin, Colombia, in August 1946.

The mission had never before sent out a children's missionary. They had never opened primary schools in other fields, for in Japan and Korea educational opportunities were different than in Colombia. To Carol's delight, she found that the missionaries in Medellin shared her desire to establish schools for the children.

Although she seemed so youthful that the missionary children loved to play games with her and listen, entranced, to the stories she told, the calendar declared that Carol had passed the missionary day of grace. According to the rules for accepting missionaries, God can call anybody into His harvest field—anybody under thirty years of age! But however impossible it might be, here she was already on the mission field, and acting very much like a missionary.

Without appointment as a missionary, without any promise for the future, without any mission support, Carol enrolled in language school. Like all missionaries from the United States, she had been reared where there is no Latin ambiguity, no elusive reflexives, no subjunctive when a rugged indicative will say what you mean. But she tackled Spanish—as every other task—gaily and determinedly. Soon she had the joy of understanding those who spoke to her, began to get her meanings across, and then in conversation with the Colombians, found an opportunity to use not only her Spanish, but her gift for gay laughter and pantomime.

The year after Carol's arrival in Colombia, the mission formed the Elementary Christian School Committee to promote Christian education for unschooled children. They went even further: they chose an able young lady—Ines Vargas—as the first Colombian teacher, and sent her to begin the Inter-American Christian Day School in Barbosa, Santander.

Carol Harding's vision was on the march; the mission had a primary school in operation. The board either had to stop it or approve it. They approved. Friends rallied to Carol's support. The board either had to approve *her* or remove her from the field. Again they approved; and there was Carol—a full-blown missionary! What a story! God *can* do anything but fail!

In 1948 the committee gave Carol a tremendous assignment for one just out of language school; they sent her to Barbosa as supervisor of the first elementary Christian school. The Colombian teacher, Ines Vargas, a gay, happy person, welcomed Carol as a beloved friend. Both were dedicated to the cause of Christian schools for Colombia's neglected children. Referring to these days, Carol said later, "It surely taught *me* a lot. I had been *such* a proud schoolteacher in the States!

"Of course it was frustrating not to see good methods and materials being used. Ines was teaching only by memorization, with the students repeating the lessons by rote. The texts were a hundred years out of date."

Carol purposed to introduce modern teaching methods by using flash cards. Ines received the suggestion very politely, but this young Colombian had no idea of taking up something so new as flash cards, especially from a person who could not speak her language fluently, and who knew so little of the customs and culture of her land.

Finally Ines proposed a solution. She said, "Senorita Carol, I will give you part of the students, and you use your methods with them." Nothing could have sounded fairer than that.

So Ines assigned to Carol all the stupid and naughty students and went merrily on her way with the others!

Relating it later, Carol said with a laugh, "Oh, what a darling Ines was! She has been my dearest friend and helper all these years!"

Carol reached Barbosa shortly before the *bogotazo,* the

revolution that burst in Bogota, and, for most historians, began *la violencia* (the ten years of special political violence). The assassination of a popular political figure and orator, Jorge Eliecer Gaitan, in Bogota on April 9, 1948, shook the entire nation. The town of Barbosa went wild.

As Carol looked out the door, she saw frightening knots of people everywhere. On the mountains just outside the town, bonfires blazed. Shouted patriotic speeches resounded from the balconies. And then, suddenly, the turmoil faded into an awful deathly silence. To her horror she saw every place of business closed, tightly locked, and the windows boarded up.

Carol operated a small boardinghouse for out-of-town students; but with no refrigeration and no place for storing supplies, she had to make daily purchases of groceries and even staples. With eleven hungry mouths to satisfy and no provision for emergencies, her situation was a bit desperate. Almost no one walked in the streets. Friends warned her to be especially careful to remain inside, for the town was furious with the United States and all North Americans.

One day when some soldiers visited the town, and things were a bit quieter, Carol ventured out. A lady opened a little grocery store just enough for her to squeeze in, and by candlelight she bought what she needed. Another day she found some firewood nearby. But the intensity of the guerrilla warfare seemed terrible.

One morning as the boarding students played in the yard, a hundred or more men, armed with machetes, guns, and clubs, ran wildly past her combination home and schoolhouse. They were chasing a man who piteously screamed, "Don't kill me! Don't kill me!"

The children, without a word, went tumbling into Carol's room, fell on their knees, and folded their hands in prayer. Carol said, "Their pretty brown skin turned a green color with fear. I had never seen anything like it before."

But despite *la violencia,* the classes continued for several years in the old hotel at Barbosa which a later missionary, John Harbison, and his wife turned into a residence, school, and chapel.

In 1949, another Colombian girl went to teach in Barbosa, and Carol returned to Medellin where she started teaching in the seminary. This was the beginning of a normal department that produced a group of noble and dedicated young men and women who went forth in unprotected isolation at the risk of their lives to establish Christian schools along the rivers.

By 1951, despite the waves of violence and terror, Carol's vision resulted in sixteen elementary Christian schools in rural areas, giving four hundred children their first chance for learning.

You may ask, What made the difference in violence occurring before and that occurring after *la violencia*? Prior to *la violencia* sporadic violence flared occasionally, just as crimes are committed anywhere at any time. During *la violencia* throughout Colombia violence was general, and even the authorities, including the police became agents of violence. This resulted in personal, political, and religious differences being settled by violence. Anyone's life could be in jeopardy at any time from individuals or from armed groups of guerrilla fighters representing two antagonistic political factions.

An incident at Barbosa illustrates the chaos of these times. Geneva De Young, a missionary, and Margarita Ortíz, a Colombian graduate of the normal department, while teaching in the Barbosa Elementary Day School, lived upstairs in a room at the St. George Hotel. About twelve o'clock one night, pounding on the hotel door awakened the young ladies. They could hear a group of men yelling that they wanted *la gringa* (the American girl)—Geneva De Young.

The drunken mayor of the city headed the group; and as all were armed, the hotel proprietor could not refuse them entrance. After gaining admittance to the hotel, to the horror of the girls, the men started tramping up the stairs to the second floor. The mayor began pushing doors open and demanding *la gringa,* or, as he sometimes called her, in derision, "*la gringa* goddess!"

Geneva and Margarita threw their whole weight against the door, determined to hold it, though the odds were so unequal. But before reaching their door, with the caprice of a drunken man, the mayor turned, went downstairs, and started drinking in a friend's room.

The girls' situation was desperate; if the mayor returned, it would be hopeless. In hope of escaping, they took off their shoes, crept down the stairs, and crawled under the hotel where the dogs and cats lived. They would have vivid memories of the hordes of fleas for many years!

At last the mayor left the hotel but returned shortly with a double-barreled shotgun and a flashlight, and began once more demanding that he be given *la gringa.* He now started a thorough search, going systematically from door to door.

A Colombian lad who worked in the hotel came to the girls where they lay hiding under the hotel and told them that they must escape immediately.

Crouching low, they crept along the rear wall, behind some bushes, then started across the patio to get to the outside door. When the girls were halfway across the patio and in plain sight, except for the darkness, the mayor stepped out from the hotel and took a few steps toward them. They stood transfixed with fright. Coming from the lights inside the hotel, the man evidently could see nothing and turned back into the hotel.

As the girls went on, silently creeping through the rear door of the patio, the same angel that closed the lions' mouths for Daniel kept the watchdog from barking. How they climbed the high wire fence that enclosed the hotel property and got over the two strands of barbed wire at the top, they will never know. At last, bruised and bleeding—it seemed like a miracle—they were able to run along the path to a thicket in which they hid.

At four the next morning, the hotel errand boy found them and said that the mayor had left the hotel and that they must come back before they were discovered by the country people, who would soon start coming to town over the trail.

Strange to say, next morning, the mayor left town for a few hours, and the young ladies boarded a train for Bogotá. When the mayor returned, he extended his search to include trains and buses, but God had taken *la gringa* and her companion out of his reach.

From the young teachers who risked peril and hardship to give bright-eyed groups of youngsters their only hope of schooling, have come congregations of church members and future church leaders.

While Carol was on furlough in the States, Geneva De Young established the George Washington School for missionary children, on the Manantiales property. Upon her return the following year, Carol took responsibility for this school. Year after year the graduates have gone on to colleges and universities, all with a splendid record of achievement. Some are now on other mission fields; and one of them, Howard Biddulph, finally returned with his wife to Colombia to serve university youth. As the George Washington School is interdenominational and inter-mission in its policy, a large spectrum of English-speaking students are enrolled.

As I sat listening to Carol's story of those years of adventure, she paused, as though thinking of God's protecting care and guidance, then said, "How marvelous!"

I waited, wondering if she had another word; then she said, "That's about all!"

Still I waited. There was another pause, another silence. Then she added, midway between laughter and tears—"Oh, I'm so glad I didn't miss it!"

14

"A Must For Eternity!"

As Marcial and his wife, Bautista del Delgado, entered Puerto Berrio's Catholic church, they touched their foreheads with holy water, then crossed themselves as they knelt. Next to them a woman was praying ardently that all the saints in heaven and the holy Virgin Mary would deliver Puerto Berrio from the Protestants.

Marcial had never heard of them before. Who could these dangerous people be? At least, like himself, they might be opposed to the kind of Colombia that had left him battling poverty in a thatched shanty along the river, and his children without an education. He decided to look them up.

A few discreet inquiries led him to the small evangelical chapel where he made the acquaintance of Rafael Meneses, who had helped to build the Manantiales seminary and was now the pastor-builder of the new church. So pleased was he with what he learned of "the new religion," that, after this, on his trips to market, he would come for more instruction in the Word, and, when necessary, accept the proferred hospitality of sleeping overnight on a bench.

Marcial Delgado, a bearded squatter living a few miles downstream on a small piece of land he had wrested from the jungle, might have been a bit vague on ideology, but he had accepted one of the very few options open to him:

he called himself a Communist. However, to keep his standing in the community, and probably with the thought of playing it safe, he continued attending the Catholic church whenever he poled his dugout up the river to Puerto Berrio to exchange bananas, papayas, mangoes, yuca, and other products for flour, beans, and rice.

When Bill Gillam learned of Marcial, he felt an urge to visit him. The only contact these forgotten people along the rivers had with an outside world was via dugout canoe.

As colonial times gave way to the Republic founded by Simón Bolívar, and it moved toward more modern days, paddle steamers cruised the Magdalena River, connecting the larger cities; and the sound of an outboard motor now and then broke the stillness along the jungle-lined shores and up tributary streams. Most of these people, however, lived and died on the riverbanks, ignoring world wars, national political battles, the social and even the sanitary, niceties of life. Few ever had the opportunity to learn to read and write; radios were unknown; to even live seemed success, and some might feel that to die was gain. Certainly anyone who served them must come to them on the river.

Pastor Meneses arranged the projected trip for Bill, and it was my joy to accompany him. We took the train to Puerto Berrio. Here we hired two *bogas*—men who pole or paddle the sluggish dugout canoes on the river, and next morning started downstream to visit the Delgado family. They were expecting us, and when we neared the clearing that marked Marcial's home, we could see waving on the bank a large red banner that said, in Spanish, "Our home is honored today by your visit!"

Marcial, the bearded, craggy-faced father, heartily greeted us, and introduced us to Señora Delgado, a plump, pleasant-faced mother, and their two sons and a daughter.

With much joy and excitement, the family escorted us down a shaded path to where, under the canopy of mango trees, a rough board table and crude benches made an outdoor dining room.

To one side, through the low hanging branches of the mango trees, we could see the small split-bamboo house they called home. Back of that, under a small patch of thatch, resting on four poles to protect it against rain, a stove of eroded mud brick, a table of twisted boards, and some earthen vessels comprised their kitchen. Smoke from the primitive stove had turned everything black, contrasting nicely with the gray thatch, the brown-yellow bamboo, the green jungle, and the blue sky overhead.

Before long, homemade wooden trays loaded with bananas, papayas, and mangoes were set before us, and we were urged to eat. Then they spread large, fresh, green banana leaves on the rough boards for dishes, and poured out on them cooked beans, rice, and *yuca* (cassava, a large rootlike starchy vegetable not too unlike parsnips). All the while we enjoyed sipping the hot *panela* water, the delightful cane sugar drink of Colombia.

In the course of the meal, I asked Señora Delgado how many children she had.

Without a moment's hesitation, nor the slightest bitterness, she answered, "Eight are living in heaven; three are dying on earth."

As Bill and I glanced at the thatched-roof hut, the blackened open-air kitchen, the signs of flooding when the river was high; felt the sharp stings of the mosquitoes that so easily penetrated trousers and shirt, and at which we slapped incessantly though vainly; realized that snakes of all kinds, sizes, and degrees of deadliness were taken for granted, and no one in the economic circumstances of the

Delgado family could possibly hope for money to buy snake serum and hypodermic needle; we understood a little of why so few of the children lived.

Before long, Bill's Spanish songs and choruses with accordion accompaniment, were delighting the family and their neighbors who came over to enjoy the unusual event. All soon caught on to the simple lyrics and joined in the singing. After a message from the Word, we knelt in prayer.

When Bill asked Marcial, who was bent low over a bench, if he wished to pray, his body shook with deep emotion, and unashamed he let his tears fall upon the dirt floor. His prayer brought assurance of forgiveness. His wife and two sons also accepted Christ that day. A daughter made her decision later in a children's service in Peurto Berrio.

The return trip from Marcial's farm to Puerto Berrio differed greatly from paddling and floating downstream. To move the heavy, sluggish dugout against the downward flow of the river, the two *bogas* stripped to the waist, cleared the prow of the canoe, and began shoving the boat upward against the swift current. Hand over hand they pushed the long poles against the river bottom and placed the other ends upon their chests. Kicking backward with their bare feet as they strained against the poles, they took two or three running steps, forcing the boat upstream. Then, quickly lifting his pole, each man in turn passed it over the head of the other, as he went to the prow; and thus, the primitive operation continued.

The heat was intense; the heavy atmosphere above the river seemed to refract the sun's rays; no breath of air reached us as we sat on the floor of the dugout. For parasols, we cut palm branches to hold over our heads.

Now and then, the *bogas*, dripping with perspiration,

dipped up the muddy water of the river, lapped it from their hand, sucking it in deliciously, saying, "Oh, this water is sweet, sweet!" It would take more than poling a dugout before Bill or I could have said that, for the city of Puerto Berrio just above us, poured sewage and dumped garbage into this river. But the Magdalena is broad, the fish are many, and it is an article of faith, despite the many towns and settlements along its length, that a river purifies itself.

This trip burned the needs of the river people into our hearts. Hundreds of unevangelized miles of a vast river system beckoned to us, but dugouts could only reach a very few of the nearby homes.

At a four A.M. prayer service in the seminary offices at Manantiales, Kenneth Haines, for some years a volunteer worker with the mission, rose to his feet and said, "The people that walked in darkness have seen a great light. That means the rivers of Colombia."

He looked at a large, colored map of Colombia that nearly covered one wall of the office. Green ink showed the rivers, the lakes and swamps which they serve, and the areas where, in high water, small boats are said to pass unhindered from the Amazon River system to that of the Colombian rivers. (This may have been an optimistic reference to short portages which connect them.)

As though God just then spoke the words Kenny had quoted concerning Colombia, he laid his hands upon the major river areas on the map, saying, "We claim them all for Christ. 'They that dwell in the land of the shadow of death, upon them hath the light shined' " (Is 9:2).

Surely this prayer was also prophecy, for prayer is not man imposing his will upon God, but rather, God revealing His will to man—calling man to share in its fulfillment.

Friends in the United States who heard of Puerto Berrio's site on the Magdalena River, sent down a small fiber glass skiff with an outboard motor—a vast improvement over sitting in the bottom of a dugout and being slowly poled by *bogas* and baked by the sun. Such archaic transportation limited the outreach to a very few miles of the great river system, and incurred a considerable loss of time and strength. The small skiff made it possible to skim over the surface of the river in a breeze created by the rapid and effortless movement.

When the Meneses' family left Puerto Berrio, Miss Florence Cavender volunteered to go there. Since 1944, Florence shared, and often led, in every phase of the mission's advance. To tell her story would be to write a history of the work.

In Puerto Berrio, Florence's home consisted of two or three small rooms built on the floor above the mission hall. Wide open verandas and walls up about a foot from the floor permitted ventilation by any breath of air that might be stirring. Accommodations of a primitive nature were at the rear, under a bamboo lean-to. It was a far cry from the beautiful Manantiales seminary grounds and buildings, but it proved that missionaries do not volunteer because of beautiful surroundings or commodious housing, but to answer the challenge of serving others.

The fiber glass skiff gave Florence an opportunity to reach out to additional families along the Magdalena. Her love for the hardy settlers and their families who pushed back into the jungle sent her in the little boat over the strange, glassy-surfaced *caños*. These small waterways, in the wet season extend for many miles back into the jungle, forming natural drains for these almost flat lands. When the dry season comes and the water is gone from the *caños,* they are used as trails.

With the outboard motor, Florence enjoyed visiting these tiny hidden settlements far out in the primeval jungle. She delighted in eating red monkey meat, sleeping in a hammock, and using visual techniques to make the message real to children and their elders; and her inspired travel descriptions were published far and wide. So interest in the river work grew.

Many needs in these isolated river communities stirred one's compassion. A strange death stalked among these thatched-roof shanties. A child apparently well in the morning might die before nightfall. Babes, laughing and cooing at twilight, were dead in the morning. Physicians knew little or nothing about the cause. Their informed guess was that prolonged inbreeding accounted for this mystery.

These river people differed from the colder, more suspicious people of the mountains. Normally, they invited visitors to share their humble food or to pass the night in their dwelling. But to stay overnight could test the vitality of one unaccustomed to clouds of mosquitoes and other biting insects; nor did one find refreshment from passing the night in a bed made by nailing or tying together twisted jungle tree limbs that left relief maps of the Andes Mountains upon one's person! Most of all the river people received the Word gladly, and enjoyed learning and singing gospel songs and choruses.

Burton Biddulph used the fiberglass skiff to make one of the earlier and shorter evangelistic probes on the river, accompanied by a Colombian evangelist and pilot. At noontime they stopped at a primitive river home to ask for *arepas,* balls of baked corn meal with very tough exteriors, and *agua de panela,* brown-sugar water.

While the woman of the house prepared these, she fell into conversation with the Colombian pilot. She confided to him, "I have three daughters. One went to live with a man who works for the oil company. My other daughter I gave to a settler down the river. I would like to give you my youngest daughter who is still with me."

"But I'm already a married man," the evangelist protested.

With a puzzled look, the lady inquired, "A married man—what is that?"

At another place, Burton began telling the story of Jesus. After listening for a few moments, the woman of the house broke in, "Oh, I have San Azulito [Little Blue Saint]; he answers all my prayers."

She went to the wall and took down what appeared to be a small ebony twig. Two bits curved upward like pleading arms. Between them a knob of black wood had been carved to give the appearance of eyes and nose. An aluminum wrapper from a cigarette pack, decorated with the colorful *pielrojo* (redskin) advertisment tied about its midriff with a piece of brown twine, gave it a primitive touch of elegance. Below the cigarette wrapper, the curious object was branched sufficiently to imagine legs.

"Where did you get this?" Burton asked.

"Oh, he came in the river one day. I fished him out and dressed him up. I pray to him every day, and he answers my prayers."

Yes, these were the disenfranchised ones, beyond Colombia's culture, civilization, or religion; their physical, mental, and spiritual needs screamed for help.

But God used—yes, consumed—John Harbison to open this great chapter of evangelical history. John, a smiling blue-eyed Irishman, spent sixteen years in Colombia before uniting with the Inter-American Mission. Part of the guidance for that decision came to him from a worn copy of the book, *Charles E. Cowman: Missionary Warrior,* which he read through a dozen times while working with another mission. He previously had served in Chinquinquirá, a city of fabled fanaticism, where old railroad ties set on end formed a barricade around his home to protect the family against stray bullets!

When John united with the Inter-American Mission, the church came with him. Almost inevitably, a man of John's evangelistic fervor found a preaching mission along the banks of the Magdalena-Cauca-Nechi River system irresistible. It would have to be irresistible, for one to attempt it in a little fiberglass skiff.

That wee boat was only a scant ten or twelve feet long; the rear portion was occupied by the motorist-pilot. For a long trip, because supplies were uncertain en route, a large drum of gasoline had to be taken. Add a box or two or tracts and gospels, an old battered valise, a briefcase with Bible and papers, and a concertina on which to play chorus tunes, and little room is left for John!

He ate occasionally at nondescript open-air spots of dubious reputation with dingy utensils and dishes. More frequently he ate at the little bamboo huts, where the bill of fare depended on the ambition of the women who cooked it, or on the supplies on hand.

Sleeping accommodations? Well, river people are amiable and cordial. Nearly always he found room on the dirt floor or a straw-over-logs bed. But difficulties or inconveniences could not deter John from any course he felt was right. These neglected river people did not have the gospel; he did. The necessity was upon him to share it. Few would have had the courage to begin such an itinerary;

only many years pioneering in Colombia conditioned him to complete it.

Upon his return John wrote a letter which burned its way into every heart. He had traveled a thousand miles on the rivers of Colombia. At every clearing or village where the little boat stopped, old and young quickly gathered. John read from the Scripture, preached, testified, and sang to the accompaniment of his concertina until, exhausted in the heat, he could not utter another sound. Still the people stood with unabated interest, as though saying, "Surely you are not going to stop now. Remember, we never heard anything like this before!"

With such audiences, John preached his very heart out at every stop. As the boat skimmed over the water to the next settlement, his strength revived sufficiently to begin again.

Where John stopped for the night he held a longer service, as people came in from nearby clearings or from across the river. Not only did they want to learn choruses, but they came to ask many questions. For John, each stop in the humid tropical atmosphere exhausted his physical reserve; for the audience, his visit meant a once-in-a-lifetime break in the monotony of their existence.

John once told of running into a school of alligators before the pilot noticed. Any of the huge beasts could have upset them or wrecked the fragile skiff, with its tail; but by slowing the boat and paddling quietly, they got through.

Where large rivers pour their waters into the Magdalena, even large boats have to use caution not to be caught in a whirlpool. At one such junction, the skiff swung around on the edge of a vortex. The momentum of the top-heavy drum of gasoline flung the boat over on its side. John said, "I was looking down into a whirlpool from which it seemed nothing could save us. Instantly I cried to God. The craft righted itself, and we sped on our way!"

Then John gathered up all the holy passion of his heart in an immortal phrase none of us had heard before: "A gospel launch for this river is *a must for eternity!*"

John's words seemed to be a divine fiat. He had seen the vast hunger of the people, the utter spiritual vacuum in which they existed. His experience told him that if men were to evangelize these riverbanks, they would have to come in a conveyance in which they could eat and sleep, in which they could remain for a campaign when opportune, and which could carry a team for evangelizing the towns. John knew that nothing less than a gospel launch could evangelize hundreds of miles of river settlements.

John's words, "A gospel launch for this river is a must for eternity!" were really his last will and testament. On that grueling trip, in the unrelenting heat, nights without rest following days of physical weariness as he lovingly poured forth the good news to those who had never heard it before, John had not only preached with all his heart but had actually preached his heart out!

Because of John's physical exhaustion after returning, he was sent to the cooler air of Bogotá. But he did not recover; his strength was gone.

For many years John had had no rest, so the mission ordered a year's furlough in the British Isles.

Three weeks after arriving in "the Old Country" with his wife and their two little ones, in the quiet home, as the sun was setting, John sat rocking gently in the fading light.

Someone entered the room and noticed that the rocking had stopped.

A smile lighted up John's face.

His journey had ended.

His lifework was complete.

In death as in life John laid upon the mission "a must for eternity!"

15

Who Built the Ark?

"I'M JUST A DRY-LAND Washington farmer who built his ark on the Magdalena River!" Eugene Wittig explained, laughing, as he thought of the tangled skein of events that put him in Colombia and, finally, in a position of worldwide missionary responsibility. Gene Wittig's story is a story of impossibilities realized.

Gene was raised in eastern Washington on his father's wheat and cattle ranch of some sixteen thousand acres. He can scarcely remember when he started riding horses. Before he got out of grade school, he could rope and brand cattle. From this he graduated to driving tractors to prepare fields for drilling wheat. Then, to cap it off, he learned to use a small airplane to keep track of the cattle in the pastures and to secure needed repair parts at distant cities, as well as for pleasure and the sport of hunting coyotes from the air.

Gene thought it was fun to repair machinery in the farm shop. Here were the drill presses, lathes, and tools to almost any machine. It took some time before he finally was allowed to wear the big goggles for electrical welding and to use the blue flame of the ethylene torch to cut through heavy pieces of steel in repairing farm equipment. It never occurred to Gene or his family that this was a missionary training school!

Ambition spurred him to enroll in Seattle Pacific College; but his heart was always back in the big ranch home out in eastern Washington, under the clear blue skies, surrounded by green fields that stretched away to the horizon, with horses to ride, and tasks he loved to do. Apparently Gene's future was pretty well determined, with both his background and his interest being in ranching. He had grown up in a Christian home, where Bible reading and prayer were taken for granted; but, all in all, the odds seemed heavily weighted toward his becoming a large farm or ranch operator rather than a minister or missionary.

With three years of college behind him, Gene's situation was "three down, and one to go." Then, before finishing the last year, he became conscious that God was talking to him.

While Gene was still away at school, a colorful missionary from Colombia, from what was then known as the Mission of the Andes, spoke in Gene's home church. He told about the farm machinery and building equipment that had been donated to the mission, but that there was no one in Colombia who knew how to set it up and keep it running. Gene's family and friends told this missionary, "If you want to get that machinery on the job and keep it moving, Gene's the man you're looking for." They even agreed that if this gentleman would go over to Seattle Pacific College and talk Gene into going to Colombia, they would pay all expenses.

When this man interviewed Gene, he described a land of gold, emeralds, and cattle out on the endless plains of eastern Colombia. *Eastern Colombia! Could that be anything like eastern Washington?* Gene wondered. The organization this man represented was appealing for men who would go to Colombia as a missionary and raise cattle—*a missionary raising cattle!* There were fortunes to be made in cattle; and large investments in mission work of all kinds were needed for schools, Bible training centers, churches, and evangelistic operations.

Gene was also intrigued by this man's colored slides. He saw Colombia's cowboys out on the plains; the killing and butchering of a steer, where everybody in the region was invited in for a feast of skewered steaks roasted before the fire; herds of cattle; and the great wide plains on which they grazed. Some slides showed the towering Andean mountains in the background; others showed the endless horizons stretching out toward Brazil. Some slides looked down from the foothills, showing the green trees that marked the courses of rivers, where very recently anacondas twenty-five feet or more in length made it risky for calves to go to the water.

Though it was difficult to secure resident visas for Colombia, the speaker was able to secure entrance for farmers, ranchers, and men with mechanical experience. Such men would have to fill the missionary gap for a nation that greatly needed the gospel.

His heart pounding, Gene Wittig listened to this appeal, his imagination picturing himself in the center of everything this speaker described. This was the life Gene knew—with exotic differences of scenery, language, and culture, all thrown in for good measure.

The speaker emphasized the fact that what he presented was a *now* challenge; there was no promise that anybody could enter Colombia tomorrow. He was appealing for qualified young men who were ready to put their heart and their fortune in their hand and say yes to God *now*.

Gene felt compelled to answer this call. It all seemed tailored to his total preparation, and he had always recognized Christ as the Lord of his life. He agreed to go down for four to six months to set up the machinery and teach others how to use it and keep it in repair. Then he would return in the fall to continue his studies at Seattle Pacific College. He applied for a passport, secured a visa for Colombia, and planned to leave April 15, 1948.

But the *bogotazo*—the riotous revolution of April 9—broke out in Bogota when the popular candidate for the presidency, Eliecer Gaitan, was assassinated in the street. The whole nation was plunged into chaos. The Colombian government advised Gene that the nation's frontiers were closed to foreigners until the political situation was normalized.

Gene expected to be cleared for Colombia within a few days or weeks at the most, but months went by without a word. It seemed that he had been following a chimera. The reasonable thing was to reregister at the college and get on with his studies. But, as always, God had charge of events.

On the last day of July, a special delivery letter brought his passport and resident visa for Colombia and permission to enter at once. By now, the first flush of enthusiasm for the venture had faded, and Gene was inclined toward first finishing his studies and graduating from college. However, upon discussing the matter with his pastor, with missionary friends, and with the head of the college's missions department, he learned that it was very unusual to obtain a resident visa for Colombia and that he should not throw away such an opportunity. Also he was young enough to go to Colombia for a period of service and return later to complete the needed studies for graduation. Shortly thereafter, he arrived in Medellin, Colombia, to register in the Presbyterian language school.

In this same school was a charming young student by

the name of Marjorie Wood. She was a registered nurse under appointment by the Presbyterian Mission to serve in Guatemala. As many single missionary girls must do, Marjorie had planned to spend her life alone in the service of the Lord. Then she met Gene Wittig.

But Gene was not "exactly" eligible: he was not Presbyterian! He was a member of a small and practically unknown faith mission—"and never the twain shall meet!"

But he *was* a very appealing young man. Marjorie couldn't deny that. And neither of them could deny their attraction to each other.

At this time, the Bible Seminary of Colombia, in its chapel at Manantiales, put on a combined singspiration and a somewhat informal Youth for Christ type of service on Saturday nights. Marjorie gladly accepted Gene's invitation to accompany him to these meetings on the other side of the valley.

After a hard week of Spanish study, they both enjoyed the relaxation of the music, and the social hour afterward in the Big House, where they could relapse into English for a time of fellowship. In some respects an ideal romance seemed to be developing, but mission boards have regulations in which the word *romance* does not occur. Imagine such a precedent! Regulations admit of no exceptions. Therefore, serious, if not insurmountable, obstacles were in the way of this acquaintance developing into a lifetime partnership.

But, as their friendship deepened, there was no harm in considering possible arrangements. Perhaps the Presbyterian board would accept them as a missionary couple. But on the application form which Gene must fill out, there were some difficult questions, such as, "What college did you graduate from?" He had not yet graduated from any college. To get under the wire into Colombia, he had left Seattle Pacific College a little too soon for that.

Then, why couldn't Marjorie join Gene's mission, and he would pay her way out of obligations that would normally only be satisfied when she completed her first term of service on the field?

But changes were occurring in Gene's mission. Difficulties in leadership of the mission caused the group of young missionaries to seek merger with some other group. Discussions were already under way with the Inter-American Missionary Society. From a legal, technical interpretation of Inter-American board rules, such a merger was impossible.

Impossible? The IMS personnel in Colombia could not accept the board's decision as final!

An important international situation pressured toward the merger: the Colombian government was refusing all visas to missionaries. The Inter-American Mission was in a more desperate situation than they knew. It would be ten years before another residence visa would be granted to one of their missionaries.

These young, aggressive, spiritual missionaries knocking on the IMS doors for admittance were among America's finest Christian young people. They had abilities needed to adequately man the Colombian field. They had the Spanish language; and beyond that, they had permanent visas for Colombia. So, what never happens, did happen. Rules were suspended; the merger was approved; and Mary Joiner, Nobie Pope, Emmabeth Hayes, the Frank Hornungs, the Stewart Sparrows, the Ignacio Guevaras, and Eugene Wittig became members of the IMS.

But that was not all. The Presbyterian Church of Medellin had such a wedding as had never been seen before. Because of it, a radiant Marjorie Wood became Mrs. Eugene Wittig and, ipso facto, a member of the Inter-American Missionary Society.

For their honeymoon, the Wittigs went to the "in" place then for vacationers—the Magdalena Hotel in Puerto Berrio. By day and by night, from the deck chairs on the wide veranda, the Magdalena River could be seen beyond a row of tall trees, reminding them constantly of the romance and adventure of past centuries, and whispering to them of a present generation waiting, hopelessly waiting, along its shores.

They enjoyed the excitement of the great river paddle steamers coming and going, whose booming steam whistles fairly made the town tremble; the shouting and laughter of the *cargadores,* stripped to the waist, running up and down the gangplanks with huge sacks of coffee, bales of cotton, and other produce, their sturdy bodies beaded with sweat; then, the whole town turning out to greet hundreds of passengers as they poured from the late afternoon train from Medellin, coming to make connections with the steamboats or to vacation in the hotel. So from the very beginning of their marriage, the Magdalena River became very much a part of Gene and Marjorie's life.

Gene and Marjorie came into the IMS at the time when "a must for eternity" on behalf of those along the Magdalena River stirred the heart of the mission. In faith, Gene was asked to study the gospel launch project and to make estimates of the cost of building one.

At once he began amassing facts. He learned that no launch could be imported from the United States. A visit to the port of Barranquilla revealed a price range, for a launch of the capacity the mission must have, from fifteen to twenty-five thousand dollars. Gene finally reported that with five thousand dollars for materials, he could build the needed launch. That is the kind of missionary mission boards seldom send to the field!

Surprisingly, in the United States the challenge of building the gospel launch brought no response. God, however, seemed to be saying, "Don't be anxious! I will provide this launch in My own way, in My own time. Only believe!"

In the Seattle Pacific College auditorium, I had been asked to address a special missionary meeting. Contingents of students came from Washington University and elsewhere to fill all seats. Life service rather than an appeal for funds, of necessity, became the theme; but I felt compelled to use John Harbison's river journey and his deathless phrase, "a must for eternity," as an illustration.

After the meeting was dismissed, an old gray-headed retired minister of the gospel came up to ask how much a gospel launch would cost. Because of Gene's research, I could tell this senior citizen that to purchase a launch might cost up to twenty-five thousand dollars but that one could be built for five thousand. Not long after this, a letter came from this minister stating that he and his wife had sold some assets and were enclosing a check for thirty-five hundred! Soon another letter brought a check for fifteen hundred! Now Gene had the challenge of delivering a launch on the Magdalena River within a budget of five thousand dollars!

Gene at once took his Colombian pilot friend and started for Barranquilla to purchase a hull on which to construct the launch. He discovered that the wartime price of hulls had been raised to nine to ten thousand! His pilot friend said, "There are often old hulls tied up along the river. Let's hunt for one, and see if we can buy it." Search as they might, the prices were too high or the hull unsuitable.

Then they heard of a boat that had recently sunk in the river. They located the owner and made arrangements to dive down and examine the craft, but the swift flow of muddy water made it impossible to make a decision. Gene then agreed with the owner to raise the boat and have first option for its purchase.

Gene found that the hull was of a good design, made by a United States manufacturer; and though the plates were rusted badly, the sturdy angle iron of the frame was in good shape. All he would have to do was to widen the frame two feet and lengthen it four feet! For Gene, with an acetylene torch, this was a simple operation. He made the purchase and arranged for the hull to be transported to a riverbank above Puerto Berrio, where the launch would be constructed.

In the meantime, Gene made another trip to Barranquilla, where he bought steel sheets for covering the hull and aluminum sheets for building a light superstructure. Though he had never worked in aluminum, theoretically he knew he could. It wasn't long until the IMS had its own "shipyard" in operation with the gospel launch under construction.

One day as Gene Wittig and his helpers worked on the launch, they looked up the river and saw something curious approaching. Two groups of buzzards were apparently floating down toward them on the water. As the great awkward birds came nearer, they were seen to be standing on and devouring two decapitated human bodies. *La violencia,* which eventually caused the death of some three hundred thousand people, had begun in the upper river communities. Fascinated, Gene and his helpers watched the bodies float past, then returned to work.

One thing Gene failed to take into consideration was that

the construction, size, shape, dimensions, and safety factors of all boats must meet rigid specifications to be approved by the government for operation on the river. Gene had observed other boats, prayed over every detail of the work, but he had never built a boat before.

Amazingly, when inspection came, all government requirements had been met. Perfect performance marked its maiden voyage in January 1951, and lighter aluminum construction made it one of the speediest boats of its size.

Gene may have been a dry-land farmer, but he had successfully built his "ark," and now was determined to learn to operate it on the river.

It took patience and endless practice to become a river pilot. Gene always had to know where the deep water ran; but with the river so muddy, it seemed there could be no way to tell deep from shallow water. Unless he could tell, he would run his ship aground, perhaps overturn it, certainly lose it. Stare and study as he would, at first Gene could not see the difference. They told him the two kinds of water differed in color; Gene saw no perceptible variations in the water's tint. They told him one kind reflected the sky more than the other; everything looked the same to him.

"But finally," Gene told me, "I began to note slight traces of difference in the coloration, a little more depth of sky reflected in some areas. Then I discovered that deep water moves faster and carries debris, sticks, and trees that the storms wash down. Shallow water has no debris on the surface. Always on a bend, the deep water naturally runs on the outside unless there are sunken rocks or some obstruction."

Gene not only succeeded in building the gospel launch and in learning to navigate it, but he revealed an intuitive way of avoiding trouble on the river. One of his adventures showed how.

Joaquin Espinoza and Gene arrived one afternoon at Montiquerra and docked the launch above the upper end of the town. Gene had been away for a time and did not know where the meeting place was nor the attitude of the people.

When he walked into town, the people said, "Oh, are you here? Don't you know there's a plot against you folks? If the gospel launch ever comes back here, arrangements are made with the inspector of police to have a mob attack you and sink the launch right here in port!"

Joaquin and Gene prayed about this a bit, and then asked where the police inspector's house was. Gene decided to go down on foot and see him. As no one had seen the launch, and most people did not know they were in town, they would surprise him.

When Gene and Joaquin went in and greeted the police chief, he stammered and stuttered and said he had orders not to permit them any type of activity because they were heretics, doing evil, and corrupting the people.

But after a bit of pressure, he was convinced that they ought to hold services right in front of his police headquarters, which faced the river, so that he could note anything they did that was out of order. Finally, he consented! In this way he became responsible for keeping order. Then the two men went back to the boat, brought it down, and tied up right in front of the police building, the most central location in town.

That night there were a couple of drunks in the crowd, and when Gene spoke, Joaquin walked down the bank with the drunks; and when he took over, Gene would steer them along the riverbank to keep them from interrupting and bothering. They had a wonderful crowd. Everybody in town was there.

Before they turned in, Gene told the police inspector good night, and as he was the first authority in the town, made him responsible for their well-being.

The next morning, the police inspector was a little more friendly. He showed them two cases of liquor that had been left with him to get the men of the town drunk so that they would be willing to carry out suggested violence against them. Never, after that, did this police chief lend himself to any type of scheming against the missionaries. As long as he was police inspector, they carried on the work in this area without a problem. But they always held services right in front of his police station!

This illustrates the uncanny rapport that Gene Wittig had with Colombians, an ability to establish smooth relations under almost any circumstance. It consisted of a combination of common sense, coolness, courage, ingenuity, faith, and a heart so filled with goodwill that it overflowed into his smile. He was so Colombian that he pointed with his nose instead of with his hand or finger! Yet, only God can explain the phenomenal growth of congregations and Christian day schools along the river despite *la violencia* that was sweeping over Colombia.

In the town of Colorado an incident occurred over which missionaries still shake their heads and laugh as they tell it, for it couldn't happen; but it did.

A group of soldiers were searching for Gene. Violence was rampant. These soldiers stopped to question a group on the street as to whether they had seen that gringo missionary Eugenio Wittig.

The Colombians shook their heads, honestly, never suspecting that the young man chatting with them was not a Colombian, but Gene Wittig in person!

With the gospel launch, there began a new and glorious chapter of missionary adventures in Colombia.

16

Seventeen Bullets

MARY JOINER was one of the young people who joined the IMS when Gene Wittig did. Exciting, dramatic things always happened around her.

You couldn't even imagine her going to the moon in a space capsule and coming back in an ordinary, monotonous splashdown in the Pacific Ocean.

No! Somehow it would be a hilarious, breathtaking story that would leave you chuckling for a week. All of life was so thrilling to her that you found yourself trembling between laughter and tears, as she told you of the drama of life about her.

While Gene Wittig and his crew of volunteer missionaries and delighted Colombians were building the "ark," Mary Joiner went to a little settlement on the Magdalena River called Carare. It was situated below Puerto Berrio, the terminal of the Medellin railroad and the river port of the department of Antioquia.

A few nights after Mary arrived in Carare, a man died. Without doctors, nurses, clinics, hospitals, or medicine, sickness along the river was usually a brief and painful prelude to death. In this case, for immediate burial, the people nailed together a narrow box of rough boards.

This death and burial struck Mary's imagination, particularly the rough, splintered, unpainted boards of the rude casket in which the dead man was dropped into a shallow grave. She saw herself, here at Carare, days away from telephone or postal service. Her death, if she became ill, could be just as swift as his, her burial as crude. She could see herself being put into a rough box and buried before anyone back home even knew she was ill!

That night, her mind filled with these thoughts, she climbed into her military hammock, protected by mosquito netting on each side, with the ends and top of canvas, zipped it tightly shut, and fell asleep.

In the night she awoke. To her dismay she was certainly in a box! She reached up her hand. Sure enough, the canvas above her felt like rough lumber. She touched the end near her head—more rough lumber! Drugged with sleep, the awful thought swept over her that she had been buried alive! She flung her arm sideways. Ah, there was the soft mosquito netting. It *was* her hammock after all! She was alive, free! Free to go on with her work!

And this is Mary's story.

While she was working in Carare, she had an opportunity to go to a neighboring town in a little dugout canoe to visit two of the Colombian teachers from our seminary's normal department. They were Isabel Soto, who came from the Barbosa congregation, and Carmen Osman, who was converted in Segovia.

While holding children's meetings there, rumors of trouble reached Mary. What they call *chusma* (armed guerrillas) were coming the girls' way. Depending on their politics, these men would kill the leaders of the village, or burn it down and destroy everyone there. It was difficult for Colombian Christians and for missionaries to be caught in this combination of political and religious tensions. Nobody knew whether this *chusma* was liberal or conservative, whether they would be for the missionaries or against them; and the answer to that question meant life or death.

The Colombian people at once began to get ready to leave. What a revelation it was to Mary, who knew of all the things North Americans have, to see these families load everything they had—absolutely everything, including their children—into one small dugout. Their houses were left absolutely empty!

It was already dark, but before shoving out onto the river they held a last evening service. These people were all new believers, for the work had just been started. Amid the songs, the prayers, and testimonies, a man stood up and said, "The Lord has given me a promise from His Word, and I feel this promise is for my family and for all our families." Then he read from Isaiah, "When thou passest through the waters I will be with thee."

Mary thought how many times she had used that verse on a card to a sick friend, or to someone who was passing through great difficulties, but that night the promise was claimed literally, just as it stands in the Bible: "When thou passest through the waters *of the Magdalena River* I will be with thee!"

The service was held in candlelight, which reflected upon their faces, and Mary could see that they were beginning to put their full trust in the Lord.

While the service was going on, shots were heard across the river, coming from a neighboring town, where Mary planned to be two days later. The people said, "They've arrived!"—meaning the guerrillas.

Then they counted the shots aloud: "one—two—three—"

The men told Mary that each shot meant a man was killed, for ammunition was scarce—one shot, one man. Slowly they counted—a total of seventeen shots. That meant seventeen political leaders of the town had been captured and shot.

As the men were making the last things ready for shoving off in their dugouts, they told Mary, "You'd better stay here. If anything happens, your people will want to know where to look for you. We'll leave two young men here. They will stay down by the shores to watch, and they'll give you notice if you need to run into the hills. Otherwise, they will stay here through the night, and in the morning they will take you out to the big riverboat that's coming through, so you can get back to Puerto Berrio."

Then they pushed out onto the Magdalena River.

Because the current is so swift and dangerous, even in the daytime the river people stay near the shore and pole their canoes. But that night, to seek a place of safety, they thrust out into the river, far from shore, some going upstream, others down—each man for himself and his family. There was uncertainty about it all; they only knew God's promise was true, "When thou passest through the waters I will be with thee," and they clung to that.

That night the three girls, Isabel, Carmen, and Mary each got into her own hammock, and each had a little bag of things ready if the boys came to call them to run up into the mountains. The girls' faith and courage was great.

A few weeks before, John Harbison had died in Ireland, only days after his arrival on furlough. Referring to him, Isabel said, "If we are killed tonight, just think, we will be the first ones to see John Harbison in heaven!"

Next morning, the two young men came up and told the girls that no wounded were brought out of the town across the river—seventeen bullets, seventeen dead!

They told the girls to get ready, and they went down by the water's edge to wait for the big paddle wheeler.

As the passenger boat came steaming up the river, the men took them out in an old dugout. The riverboat was pushing a large barge with soldiers who were being sent to quell the violence. As this canoe came alongside, the soldiers pulled them up onto the barge, and the canoe slipped away.

The three girls were dirty. The night before, in the rush of the families leaving, they hadn't left in Mary's dugout any of the little gourds that they use for dipping up the water that seeps in and covers the bottom of a canoe. So the girls had been sitting in that dirty water in the bottom of the canoe. They didn't quite fit in with the New Year's holiday crowd that was on the big paddle wheeler!

The girls had cause to praise the Lord for the opportunity of giving their testimony to those soldiers and to the passengers. They were all crowding around asking what had happened, who these girls were, and where they were going. They were especially curious to see a tall North American blonde in the crowd!

So while violence swept across Colombia, creating an inferno of hate, Evangelicals were increasing; for, as they were driven from their homes or farms, even as the disciples of old, "They went everywhere preaching the gospel."

17

Teeth and Souls

FOR SOME TIME, the crew of the gospel launch *El Cruzado* heard strange tales of the river town Galindo. It was rumored that the townspeople had destroyed a nearby village by killing its inhabitants and burning it to the ground. Such things happened frequently enough as to make the story plausible. A band of the *chusma* (guerrillas) were thought to be operating out of the town, raping, burning, killing in the undeclared civil war that was ravaging Colombia's once proud democracy.

The first time *El Cruzado* anchored in front of the stately palm that marked the location of this obscure river town, Galindo, an adventure began much greater than the gospel team then dared to dream. Beyond the palm tree, Galindo's few rambling streets ended in the jungle that ceaselessly pressed in from the hill that buttressed it from the land side. In this heat-ridden region, the split bamboo houses with thatched roofs and the two or three little country stores with faded whitewashed fronts were nothing unusual. As *El Cruzado* swung up against the riverbank and came to rest, the townspeople viewed the newcomers not only with indifference but with decided suspicion, even what seemed hostility. Doubtless they had heard weird tales of the "heretics" who operated the *El Cruzado*.

Apart from the launch it would have been impossible to

contact this hidden river town; and apart from a young lady named Nobie Pope, it is doubtful if this contact could have been successful.

Nobie had been brought to South America through the same magnetic appeal that brought Gene Wittig into the Inter-American Mission. She was a fearless Texan who loved adventure, felt deeply for those who suffered, and was ready to die for the love of Christ.

Of technical importance, she was a dental assistant, knew how to administer Novocain and how to use "lifters" in extracting offending molars. She did not know that the settlers along the rivers had not yet seen a dentist and that and there would be a gospel launch in her future. But "just in case," she brought her dental tools along. Nearly everywhere are people who need to have a tooth pulled now and then!

Of course she had to give up a professional career to the strong disapproval of some who were close and dear to her. But that was a small price to pay for the joyful assurance that God guided her life. Her friends back home felt she was throwing her life away. But only with one's life can the saying of Jesus be fulfilled, "Whosoever he is of you that forsaketh not all that he hath, cannot be my disciple" (Lk 14:33).

After launch pilot Frank Hornung carried a folding table from the boat and set it up under the palm, placed a chair beside it, and carried up a black bag, Nobie started taking out hypodermic needles, Novocain, and all the paraphernalia of a dentist. The town's curiosity was so strong that adults joined the children and young people as they crowded around to see for themselves what all this meant. Could this woman be a magician perhaps? Was she going to put on some kind of a show?

Then Nobie turned toward the crowd with a smile, as she said in Spanish, "Does anybody have a toothache?"

The people laughed. Did anybody have a toothache? *Everybody* had a toothache. Toothaches were part of existence. Most people were used to having their teeth rot down to the gums and then the last piece of the root agonizingly decay away. When the teeth were gone, the gums would harden a bit so they could munch soft food.

Nobie went on encouragingly, "If you have a tooth that is bothering you, I can remove it without pain."

Remove teeth without pain! They had never heard of such a thing. If the devil himself offered to do that, they would give him a chance to prove it. The more daring members of the group pushed forward, some holding an aching jaw, others pointing to where the painful teeth were.

At once Nobie began her "assembly-line dentistry." Quickly she blocked nerves by injecting Novocain into five or six men and women who were willing to be first. Then she started getting the teeth out. Sometimes there was a whole row where the tooth structure was so ruined she could practically scrape it away. "Lifters" got roots out. Her patients soon left the chair spitting blood, but yelling that the pain was gone.

With a deliciously professional *clink*, Nobie dropped the extracted teeth into a glass jar. To the people it sounded like putting a magical period to pain. Before long, as the jar filled, teeth dropped in without sound. In one day, Nobie recorded one hundred seventy-five teeth pulled!

Now, patients began elbowing their way toward the head of the line. Who cared that the winsome, *simpática señorita* quoted Bible verses in Spanish? She could have talked Chinese and made them like it! Who cared that she gave them "a little book," sometimes a tract with a pretty picture, and spoke sweet words about Jesus!

From the first appearance of the *El Cruzado*, one storekeeper stood in front of his place of business staring, almost glaring, at the newcomers. They learned later that his son led the guerrilla gang that ravaged, looted, burned, and killed. As he watched Nobie at work, he had to admit that here was someone helping people that never had been helped before.

Gradually the old storekeeper came closer better to see what magic this American senorita used. The people whose aching teeth had been removed laughed with relief as they told others how easy it was. These people were the storekeeper's neighbors. He knew they were telling the truth.

This old gentleman heard the words Nobie spoke. They were comforting words, they were words about a heavenly Father who sent His Son Jesus to die for the worst of sinners. Then there were short moments of prayer in the name of Jesus.

When the glass bottle was filled with teeth, and the dental equipment had been removed, gospels were distributed to everyone. The old storekeeper took a gospel and put it in his pocket. He even listened respectfully to the service that followed. This brave, winsome, American young lady had been right about painlessly removing his people's aching teeth; could it not be that she and her companions might be right about Jesus, the great Physician, who could cure the deep ache in every lonely heart?

Who did not need help these days? They all knew about poverty, violence, fear, sudden death! No one knew as he blew the candle out at night that he would see the light of another day. And religion? Well, some years, not even the priest came by to hear confessions, absolve, baptize, and marry those whose squeamish consciences prodded them to such conformity. He must admit that these visitors had been very kind. He would read their "little book."

Next morning many in Galindo who were suffering from an epidemic of pinkeye came seeking help. As Nobie administered argyrol drops, a man came leading a blind woman by the hand. After a brief examination, Nobie felt that this woman's eyes were beyond medical aid. She called to the captain of the launch, and together they prayed for the woman's healing, remembering, "If two of you shall agree on earth as touching any thing that they shall ask, it shall be done for them by my Father, who is in heaven" (Mt 18:19).

When *El Cruzado* pulled away from the shore, the crusade team knew that they had sought to serve in the name of Jesus, and that, as best they knew how they had planted the incorruptible seed, the Word of God by which men are born again. They trusted that the Spirit would use it according to the will of God.

About a month later, *El Cruzado* again reached Galindo in time for an evening service. A large, quiet crowd gathered and listened intently to the music, the songs, and the sermon. At the conclusion many came to purchase a Bible or New Testament and kept the team busy answering questions.

About midnight, a little woman, whose eyes had been relieved with argyrol at the previous visit came timidly with a gift—some *yuca*, a common root vegetable (cassava), all she had to express her appreciation. Nobie asked about the blind woman for whom they prayed on the previous visit.

The little woman replied, "Oh, the blind woman. She can see now! She attended the service tonight, but has already gone home."

Then Nobie and the team knew why they had such a large and attentive audience. When God works, people listen.

A visit with the formerly hostile storekeeper revealed that he had read the gospel and was now a believer. In fact he asked them to pray for his son who was the leader of the *chusma* that ravaged, burned, and killed.

With the continuing visits of the launch, before long the believers in Galindo built their own rustic house of worship. Then they asked for a teacher to start a school, and one of the Colombian girls, trained in Carol Harding's normal department, went to take charge. This young lady was also active as leader for a prayer and Bible study group of believers.

As converts increased in the settlements along the rivers, thirty to forty preaching points developed, and the visits of *El Cruzado* came farther apart. Severe periods of violence also interfered with the regular scheduling of the launch. On one occasion, the launch was commandeered by the military; but prayer was answered and the boat was returned.

Despite a century of developing political hatreds that at last exploded in violent action, the ministry of the launch continued. Of course men turned these chaotic days to the benefit of interests that they represented. This was even true of religion.

One such action was the missions' treaty, which the government of Colombia and representatives of the Vatican signed on January 29, 1953. This gave the Roman Catholic church exclusive rights to establish and conduct schools and to hold public religious services in all "Indian territory."

The missions' treaty assumed that Indians inhabitated

nearly two-thirds of Colombia. Actually, few countries in Latin America proportionately have as few Indians as Colombia! But the treaty included most of the river territory and placed it off bounds for evangelical missions!

Gradually evangelical schools and churches in "Indian Territory" were closed; some with violence and fire, others by the apparent legality of locking and sealing the premises. For Colombian teachers, it was heartbreaking and unbelievable that their own beloved Colombia, by government action, took Colombian children who were climbing up out of the darkness of illiteracy for the first time, and doomed them to return to that despair.

Yet, the greater the opposition the more the work grew, for it depended not upon church buildings, schools, or even ordained ministers, but upon the witness of young and old whose lives were changed. No power, either religious or political, could keep track of where all the little dugout canoes went, nor keep watch on the jungle trails as to who traveled them. Violence caused the believers to go farther with their message.

So the gospel seed was planted, the Bible did its intended work, the Word created groups of believers; and they, through the power of the Spirit continued the pattern of first-century Christians.

God had begun a good work in Galindo, how would He "complete it unto the day of Jesus Christ"?

18

Lightning Institutes

To PREPARE Christian youth along the rivers to stand firm under violence, the *El Cruzado* team started *cursillos* (little study courses). For a day, sometimes a weekend, the team taught the rudiments of Bible study, personal evangelism, and some new choruses. Evidently more was needed. To meet the challenge, Lightning Bible Institutes were developed, requiring three weeks of intensive work.

If you had accompanied the team for a Lightning Institute, your diary might have read:

Upon awakening in the hotel to shouts and laughter and Spanish talk, as our team started the day, it was still dark outside. Here, the sudden tropical sunrise of equatorial lands does not come until six o'clock. Breakfast out of the way, we started through town to where *El Cruzado* waited at the riverbank.

In anticipation of the new day, the men who move merchandise, freight, and baggage through the town were beginning to stir in their two-wheeled homemade carts, which they powered themselves. To protect these and to save the cost of living quarters, the men use them for a bed. This is not only cheaper but cooler than sleeping in a room. After being in a hot, stuffy hotel room all night under a mosquito net, I almost envied the men their open-air sleeping privileges. For this hot zone, the only better sleeping accommodation than the boards of these awkward wheelbarrows is to find a slab of concrete or cement which is always cooler than wood, or, perhaps, a cement wall that one can lie atop of and catch any whisper of a breeze from off the river. The men who had already found work were rattling the two iron wheels of their carts over the cobblestones, while others were stretching themselves or rubbing their eyes. The main street was filled with vendors' stalls set up for market day, while women looking for early bargains gathered around them.

By now the sun, peering above the horizon, was turning the dark mystery of the not distant jungle a daylight green.

As always, buzzards sat in rows on top of the buildings watching the people coming and going, as though they had some secret premonition! These ungainly creatures, they tell me, are really a boon to the city. They are the sanitation department and do most of the street cleaning. With great dispatch, they take care of dead cats, dogs, even a donkey or horse.

I clambered aboard *El Cruzado* with the pilot-engineer, the missionary teachers from the Manantiales Bible Institute and Seminary, and some students who came along to help and to learn by experience.

After committing ourselves and the launch to the care of our heavenly Father, the motor was started, and we began cutting through the glassy surface of the river, which appeared to be nearly a mile wide. As the boat picked up speed, it was pleasant to feel upon one's face the breeze this created; for already we were perspiring, though the day had scarcely begun.

Suddenly the launch's motor was cut to a bare idling speed. I wondered why, for there was nothing unusual around us, such as floating trees which storms bring down.

Then someone pointed across the water to a very small dugout. The man who was paddling it barely had room to squeeze in between the two sides. It was heavily loaded with bunches of bananas and plátanos, piles of yuca root, sacks of fruits and vegetables on their way to market. He must have been an optimist, for the edges of the loaded canoe appeared almost even with the surface of the water. To have maintained the *El Cruzado's* speed might have swamped this man's canoe.

This lone Colombian had the right of way. Centuries before motor boats arrived, dugouts like his were taking produce to the Indian markets. This man and the settlers before him had a prior right to the rivers which served as the first highways of Colombia. Beside this, the considerations of humanity dictated that we take care not to wreck this frail craft on which a man's livelihood depended.

A little later, as we swung away from sandbars standing out of the water at this dry season, men with little more than a loincloth were shoveling the washed gravel into dugouts, to be sold in a river town which was struggling from split bamboo and thatched-roof houses toward brick walls and tile.

Where the river divided to pass around the two sides of an island, our launch took the quieter water in the smaller branch. Before long, wooden floats on the surface showed where young men had anchored fishlines by wading out into the muddy water. The prize they sought was the large fish called *bagre,* which furnishes much of the protein for river people.

At Los Patos and Galindo, we stopped to pick up delegations of young people who were going to attend the Institute. They were not strangers to the gospel. Their lives had been transformed by the Word of God. They had sung the gospel at their nets, as they pounded out the chaff from the rice, as they carried their waterpots down to the riverside, or as they pounded the washing clean on rocks in the streams. Even the smaller children, as they ran to and from school with their homemade chairs carried expertly on their heads, had sung the gospel choruses.

They piled onto *El Cruzado's* decks' sleeping mats and hammocks, cartons and boxes, bags of rice, big stems of bananas, heaps of plátanos and yuca. A few of the boys swaggered a bit with broadrimmed sombreros, woven in festive colored straw of striking design.

When we rounded the last bend and the village of Colorado came into view, most of the townspeople apparently waited to welcome us. All at once they broke into a native hymn, the words and music mingling with the muffled sound of the motor. Then, as the boat came to rest beside the bank, those on board answered back with a joyous hymn of praise and thanksgiving.

The classroom for the Lightning Bible Institute was Colorado's bamboo church. The floor was tramped dirt. The desks were backless benches; Bibles and notebooks were balanced on one's knees. But the finest Bible Institute in America could not have had a more reverent, interested, and enthusiastic group of students.

Gene Wittig directed the Institute, handled logistics, and taught a class on practical Christian living. Mary Joiner made a class in personal evangelism a thrilling and happy experience. Don Felipe Barajas, an experienced pastor, helped us live the epistle to the Philippians; while Ana Sixta Guevara caused us to feel the awe of the disciples, as they followed Jesus in the gospel according to Mark. The daily program was rounded out by a class in hygiene that attempted to explain the mysterious reason why people from the United States want to boil their drinking water! The singing class, where new songs and choruses were introduced, was the high point of the day.

The Institute blended into the regular evening church services, and the congregation came to the classes on the other nights. As the Colombian youth excel in memorization, they learned at least twenty-five scripture portions to carry away in their hearts. The program on the final night not only packed out the church, but left crowds listening outside the bamboo walls.

Next morning, after the last prayer, the last song, the last *abrazo,* the last shouted adios, *El Cruzado* started on the return trip.

One last tremendous obstacle waited to test our stamina. Toughened by battling for everything they have, they were not dismayed by an immense floating island of tangled water plants and marsh grass spread out like a great green field blocking our way.

Young men with machetes went to the bow of *El Cruzado,* where they hacked and cut at the rubbery mass, while others pushed it apart with poles to make way for the craft. As the motor was stopped every few minutes, another group of young men at the rear, dove into the river and removed the water plants from the propeller. Repeated endlessly in the torrid heat of a broiling sun, this was work to daunt the strongest.

Six miles of this put us on the main river again, headed for the villages where the youth delegations left us, singing, shouting, laughing happily.

The Lightning Bible Institute brought joy to river youth, and also created a deeper hunger for the Word than it could satisfy. This was encouraging—new problems bring challenges toward new solutions.

19

Crisis Is Opportunity

FOR TWO YEARS *la violencia* made it impossible for *El Cruzado* to reach Galindo. When the gospel launch once more anchored along the riverbank not far from the stately palm that marked the town's location, as the crew and team members jumped from the deck to the riverbank, sturdy arms of Christian youths were stretched out from the shouting, laughing throng to receive them and embrace them in the love of God that continued to unite them.

The young people surprised the missionaries by asking if they might put on an Easter program. That night the *El Cruzado* team and crew had the joy of sitting in the congregation and *listening*. The fast-moving presentation amazed them. The young people quoted not only verses, but entire chapters of the Bible; their testimonies of adventures for Christ were thrilling, and their freedom of expression a delight.

After the program, the missionaries asked, "How did you learn to do this?"

The young people answered, "When the authorities shut our church and school and would not let us hold services in Galindo, we memorized songs and chapters from the Bible. Then we would leave our hymnbooks and Bible at home, and go in our canoes to a small stream back in the jungle, where nobody could find us. You should have heard us out there as we sang and testified and quoted Scripture and preached to each other. Then we would go by twos or threes to visit the families up and down the riverbanks. On the trails back into the jungles where the far out settlers live, we waded through mud clear up to our knees."

During the two years the missionaries could not reach them, God by His Spirit had taken over. The young people of Galindo had been single-hearted enough to obey the impulse of the Spirit in their heart, and in doing that, they were living out new chapters of the Acts of the Apostles.

Upon another visit to Galindo, when the tensions had mounted again, and no public service could be held, the young people came with a dramatic air of secrecy to request the *El Cruzado* team to come after dark and without flashlights to the rear of a home situated near the jungle.

When the missionaries arrived at the appointed hour, the only light was from the moon; the river flowed silently a short distance away, and the jungle at their back seemed asleep. Here were about forty-five of the village young people. Prudence forbade music or singing, but after a quiet prayer, each of the youth expressed a desire to be a preacher of the gospel or a Christian teacher. In this crowd of quiet, earnest youths sitting in the moonlight, the missionaries knew they faced what missions and missionaries are all about: youth dedicated to take the message of Christ to their own people.

Without doubt, these young people whom the Spirit of God had made new creatures in Christ, were the ones who would have to evangelize the river areas. They knew, understood, and talked the language of these people whose lives were bounded by the battle to wrest from the jungle a place for their homes; from the rivers, fish for their tables; and from the ground, rice and *yuca*. All that these young people asked was a deeper knowledge of the Bible so they could better spread the good news of a living Christ. They wanted enough training to bring reading and writing to the flocks of children and the gospel to the children's parents. As the missions' treaty made it illegal for evangelical missionaries, pastors, or teachers to enter here, these Colombian youth were the best, in fact, the only hope of a continuing advance in the river communities.

This was a crisis which the present facilities of the mission could not meet. The seminary, though excellent for its purpose, could not meet the needs of these young people. Most had had but a few months of schooling; a few, a year or two at the most. The gap between them and the seminary level of instruction was impassable.

And so this crisis of opportunity became a vision of something new, a training center in the river area, something never attempted before in Colombia, a vocational and Bible study program in a place where these young people would feel at home and could go from what they were toward what they hoped to become.

God had called to the ministry dozens of brawny young people in the river lands and other isolated areas. Living in primitive conditions, their iron muscles were their only means of livelihood. Though they may have read haltingly and written as second graders, their hearts burned with the love of God. Their sacrifice for Him and their endurance of persecution outdid anything missionaries had known. They challenged the mission to give them Bible training without robbing them of their Christian virility.

The accomplishment of this vision began with the appointment of Gene Wittig to begin scouting for a site. It had to be close to the rivers and the people with whom the prospective students would be working. Gene suggested a farm where the students could work to finance themselves while studying, and learn the skills necessary to assist them in their future support. In this way students would be prepared to communicate the Christian message while demonstrating better poultry culture, or new farming methods on their own parcel of land; others would do this as they fished or harvested with their neighbors, or helped them build a house from the materials which the jungle furnished in abundance. Some would be prepared to teach small groups of children in homes, others to be leaders of church groups; those with certain God-given abilities would raise up congregations; all would be infiltrating the river communities with the Christian message.

The place Gene chose for establishing the Vocational Bible Institute was Cristalina. It is a whistle-stop on the railroad between Medellin and Puerto Berrio, consisting of a small depot, a store, and a few scattered houses; but numbers of farms and cattle ranches are found in the area. It is only one hour away from the river port of Puerto Berrio, and, if the train arrives on schedule (a hazardous assumption), seven hours from Medellin.

Gene purchased one hundred seventy acres of undeveloped rolling hills back of the railroad station on which a spring gave ample water for the school's needs. It took someone with vision and practical experience to see in that jungle wilderness of trees and tangled vines a Bible school supporting itself with farming and husbandry.

The location of the Vocational Bible Institute at Cristalina was ideal in a number of ways: there were nearby farms, river villages, towns, and settlements to be evangelized, and here students could continue the type of Christian work they were accustomed to. In the opposite direction, the train passed through many conservative towns and cities, whose resistance to the gospel would toughen student spirit and sharpen their approach.

As though to emphasize the need for such a training center, unusual violence flared along the river areas in the spring of 1956. The government issued orders that all Protestant pastors and teachers must leave the missions' treaty territory within forty-eight hours.

On April 6, Christian workers Joaquin Espinoza and Noe Martinez were jailed in Palomino for several weeks. The stocks that held their feet, the filthy prison, the broiling sun, the abundance of gnats, mosquitoes, and crawling things made this an agonizing punishment.

In May, the entire Cauca River was closed to missionary activity. It was clear that God had timed the establishment of the Vocational Bible Institute in anticipation of these repressive measures.

As the activities of *El Cruzado* were now difficult, in many places impossible, the gospel launch was sold and the funds used to develop the grounds and buildings of the VBI training center. Youth groups raised up by the *El Cruzado* made the Vocational Bible Institute necessary. Now, through the money received from its sale, the gospel launch fulfilled the original vision of a continuing investment for river evangelism in the only way it could be carried on—by trained Christian youth of the river communities.

To confirm this decision, the railroad began to extend its lines along the river; the government began building roads into the river communities; bus service began giving easier access to towns previously reached only by river travel. Of a truth, "All things work together for good to them that love God" (Ro 8:28).

Early in 1956 the first land was cleared and plowed, the first building begun, and experiments in farming started. This, in spite of a worsening political situation. Guerrilla warfare continued near the Institute, and most of the surrounding farms were closed because of atrocities. But at "Oasis," as they called the Institute farm, materials and personnel continued to pour in.

In June, two hundred fifty baby chicks came, the beginning of what would become scientific egg production. In September, a contingent of thirty-two boys enrolled as the first student body. Always, only space and funds have limited the number of students. Today VBI enrolls one hundred students, but each year a hundred or more must be refused for lack of room.

Today, a concrete and cement feeding and milking station provide for a growing herd of cows: and a mechanical department operates under the direction of husky Julian Ramirez, a convert from Puerto Berrio and a mechanical genius. He teaches male students how to take down an automobile or launch motor to its last bolt and rebuild it in good working order. For a country where old automobile and marine motors "never die," but through the decades very gradually "fade away," this is invaluable.

Gene Wittig learned something of the real meaning of the Vocational Bible Institute when he visited a congregation that he renamed "the do-it-yourself-church!" It is in Plan de Armas, a rural area of scattered houses, forming neither village nor town, eight hours by horseback from the nearest bus stop, straight up and over three-thousand-foot mountains. In the early years of *la violencia,* five people were beheaded here. Later, numbers of Christian families migrated to this region, and Vocational Bible Institute students visited here regularly.

Gene found here a congregation of one hundred forty people, a new chapel, a school building, thirteen candidates for baptism, and forty-seven children to be dedicated. He was privileged to assist in the ceremony which made this the twenty-third organized church of the Inter-American Church Association. He wrote that these people "built a community where there is no saloon, few people smoke, and life is simple and honest. (Doors are never locked, which is unheard of in Colombia.)" Without a pastor, God used laymen and students alone to do this!

Early in the history of the Vocational Bible Institute the students chose and sent out a student missionary, supported by offerings of students and faculty. Each year this ministry has been continued.

A group of Christian young people, in the moonlight at Galindo, challenged the *El Cruzado* team; the mission answered by founding the Vocational Bible Institute. Only Gene and Marjorie Wittig and those who worked closely at their side, know the sacrifice and grinding hard work this cost. But today everyone rejoices in the results—two out of three pastors of all the Inter-American Churches are Vocational Bible Institute graduates!

20

What God Can Do

Lopez Jaramillo was only one of many who desired to fulfill a call to the ministry. Like many others, he had tremendous potential. A great forward step in ministerial training was taken when the Bible Seminary of Colombia became the *United Biblical Seminary of Colombia,* thus fulfilling the long-cherished dream of those who founded this educational center in 1944. But even this did not solve the problem of a man like Lopez who had the responsibilities of a wife and family.

The Jaramillo family was wealthy, and so Lopez had studied in Colombia's best schools. He was a graduate of Manizales College. His plans included further education in Europe's universities, but a marriage contrary to his father's wishes resulted in Lopez being disowned and cut off from all support or inheritance. His life shows that God knows how to use even disappointments.

A religious tract fluttering in the rack of a bus in which Lopez and his wife were riding, resulted in her conversion to the gospel.

Lopez, however, was another matter. During the fatal illness of his firstborn son, he had not had sufficient income to obtain needed medical attention. In bitterness of heart he had cursed God for the boy's death. But he could not deny the change in his wife.

He would say to her, "Ofelia, what is bothering you? What are you praying for?" And she would answer, "I am praying that you will be converted." Finally her prayers were answered, and he also accepted Christ as Saviour.

A few years had passed, and several children had come to the Jaramillo home before Bruce Hess of the Inter-American Mission met Lopez. Bruce was praying for someone to help the church association get gospel work established in the difficult town of Sopetran.

Previous to this, Ernesto Durango, a well-to-do baker in the city had become an Evangelical, but he and his family were driven from the town because of their religious convictions. To enter Sopetran with gospel work would require a man of experience and of unusual qualifications. It was felt that Jaramillo was such a man and had the courage to accept the challenge.

Groups of believers in surrounding areas made it impossible to have a permanent evangelical work in the trading center of this region. When they secured Ernesto Durango's former home and bakery, this gave a strategic downtown location in which to live and begin the work. Soon after moving here, Lopez Jaramillo had a Sunday school to which believers and friends from the surrounding communities began coming. Gradually some from the town of Sopetran also began to attend.

Lopez had another problem in accepting the Sopetran appointment. Though he had a good general college education, he had no theological or biblical training. With a growing family and no money, residence study in the seminary was impossible. As though anticipating Jaramillo's need, the year he accepted the challenge to go to Sopetran, the United Biblical Seminary of Colombia began a pilot project, using a new method in ministerial training. It was originated by Dr. Ralph Winter, and was called Theological Education by Extension.

With this the seminary could now reach beyond the single young men who were the usual resident seminarians and began training the natural leaders who already were serving the churches. This thrilling innovation opened the door of ministerial training to professional men: doctors, dentists, lawyers, accountants; to businessmen: heads of corporations, managers, cattlemen, land owners, technicians; yes, and to fishermen, to farmers, to workmen who desired to serve God and in whom the local congregation recognized gifts and leadership abilities. To help all these whom God calls to the service of the churches, studies were offered on four scholastic levels.

In the nationwide World Vision Pastors' Conference at the United Biblical Seminary of Colombia in April 1967, this program was launched for Ecuador, Venezuela, and Panama, in addition to Colombia. Rev. Wallace Rehner, dynamic dean of the seminary, was elected executive secretary. Dr. Ralph D. Winter wrote of this new venture,

> The unique thing in the Colombian situation is what appears to be the development of a nationwide interdenominational seminary involving already nine denominations. In most other countries this kind of triumph in cooperation has rarely even been discussed. The new structure is a tribute to the diplomacy and goodwill of the Oriental Missionary Society, which from the first intended the United Biblical Seminary in Medellin to serve all evangelical churches.*

The tremendous import of this development may be

***Theological Education by Extension* (South Pasadena, Calif.: William Carey Library, 1969), p. 209.

realized by noting that throughout Colombia, as generally in Latin America, the proliferation of congregations has been so rapid that only one in five pastors has had Bible institute training. Traditional institutions have not been able to supply trained ministers for more than a fraction of new church groups.

When Wally Rehner was asked to expand the work of the United Biblical Seminary to include Theological Education by Extension, he enrolled Lopez Jaramillo as one of the first students. This enabled Lopez to live with and care for his family while preparing himself for the ministry of the Word. It would have been impossible if he had had to become a resident seminary student, for neither he nor the mission could have afforded this, and it would have taken several years from the service which he was rendering. He was a man of intelligence and of sufficient educational qualifications to undertake the topmost level of seminary training. And now he could secure it.

A thrilling climax to setting up the TEE program came for Wally when Jaramillo asked him to go to Sopetran and assist in a baptismal service. Together with the candidates for baptism, they had the joy of walking some two miles out of the city to the river where the service was held. Several hundred people of the community also accompanied them and watched the ceremony without any disturbing incident.

Who were these courageous believers? For a partial answer meet one valiant little lady by the name of Rose Angel. She lives on the other side of a rugged mountain range. It requires a brisk four-hour walk—mountain climbing all the way—to bring her to church, eight hours round trip to be present in Sunday services. For her, that is nothing compared to the joy of fellowship with other believers, an opportunity to sing the hymns of praise, and to hear the preaching of God's Word.

Her husband was living when she was first converted. While he did not follow Rose in her step of faith, neither did he forbid her attendance at church. But when she broached the question of baptism, he said, "As long as I live, you can never be baptized." After his death she was freed from this prohibition and became a baptized member of the Sopetran church.

It was hard to imagine that this frail little widow could scratch a living out of the rugged terrain of her farm. Sometimes, she told us, things were stolen when she was away at church; but that was a small price to pay for the joy of hearing the Bible read and the sermon preached, and of singing the gospel songs.

When the last song was sung, and the last cup of coffee was drunk with Pastor Jaramillo and his wife, Rose Angel took off her shoes—worn only in church—and started out over the rocky Andean mountain trail for her home. She simply couldn't think of wearing out her Sunday shoes on such trails as those!

Lopez Jaramillo was only one of one hundred fifty-six men—the first group—helped by Theological Education by Extension, as it began to enlist teachers and students on an interdenominational basis under the aegis of the United Biblical Seminary of Colombia. The students now serve in ten denominations.

In the seminary's darkest days of testing, Mrs. Cowman wrote, "I am praising the Lord! I hope it all goes to ashes. Then we shall see what God can do!" It seemed to have gone to ashes. *La violencia* closed the seminary for a year.

But today Mrs. Cowman's unwavering faith is being rewarded: we are only beginning to see what God can do!

21

The Kunas Are Coming

FLORENCE CAVENDER was always thrilled by the romance and beauty of the jungle. The courage and fortitude with which settlers conquered it stirred her. Hers was a frontier spirit and a strength that enabled her to tackle the disciplines of a missionary's life—language study, child evangelism, pastoring a church, river evangelism, establishing Christian day schools, teaching in the Bible Seminary and the Vocational Bible Institute—all done thoroughly well, with zest, and to the glory of God.

In the gospel launch's early explorations, in a wilderness of lagoons and waterways where maps do little good, by a quiet hidden expanse of clear water, the *El Cruzado* crew made what for them was an amazing discovery—an Indian village, a remnant of the ancient Indian empire so ruthlessly destroyed by the conquistadores. These Indians wore golden earrings, such as tradition mentions. About the boat, flocks of Indian children—naked, except for their golden earrings—chattering, laughing, churned the water like a school of glistening brown fish. Florence felt a yearning to serve and help this remnant of a people lost to history.

This company of Indians, suddenly stepping out of the pages of the past, set Florence's heart afire with a new purpose which she hid in her unspoken prayers of her quiet time. Someday God would help her serve the Indians out there beyond the frontiers of Colombian life as she had known it.

When students from the Vocational Bible Institute first penetrated the far northern arm of Colombia lying along the eastern border of Panama, they found the Kuna tribe in Arquia. Florence wondered what the story they brought back meant for her. The setting amid the deep jungle delighted her; the needs of the people overwhelmed her. The new diseases white settlers brought as they pressed nearer to the Indian village spread death among them. To hear of a young boy suffering from the "plague" of measles, burning with fever, carried down to the river, and plunged into its cold waters, only to die of pneumonia a few hours later, broke her heart. The welcome the chief gave the students seemed like the voice of the Lord bidding her go. Even the difficulties of the way were a challenge to dedicate her strength and will, her devotion and courage, to serve these whom the onrush of civilization had so callously brushed aside.

Word came that the chief's wife was very ill. The medicine man had fastened to her hammock skulls of many different kinds of animals. Underneath the hammock, in addition to hundreds of little wooden gods, outward symbols of their religion, he had placed a gourd filled with a brew made from the thorny barks of trees, and another gourd filled with plant juices in which to bathe. Intermixed with his incantations, he used smoke, songs, and bloodcurdling yells. His services seemed to insure a speedy death.

In the tribal meetings, one man after another went through a strange performance. One would rise and begin talking slowly, then faster and faster, louder and more furiously, until, his body writhing, the perspiration trickling from his bronze skin, he would reach a climax of frenzy, then drop exhausted, to be followed by another.

Fortunately, evangelical believers, driven out of their homes by persecution and violence had come to this area near the Indians to establish the village of Gilgal. To the Indians' glad surprise, they found that these settlers were not seeking either their women or their land. They also began to observe the kindness and love manifested among members of the Christian families.

When Carlos Oliveros, one of the Vocational Bible Institute students, visited Gilgal, some of the Christian community led him back far into the jungle toward the Indian village. From a great distance they could hear loud shrieks and cries, the beat of drums, and the tap of feet. As the visitors came nearer, they saw a group of dancing Indians surrounding a grass hut; and before the hut were many wooden figures representing their gods.

As the chief came forward to welcome his Christian neighbors and greet Carlos for the first time, he told them, "Gabriel, one of our finest boys, has just been bitten by a snake. His leg is swelling. He will die."

"No. He will not die," his evangelical friend said, impulsively. "I know where I can get some medicine to cure him."

Then he turned to Carlos as he asked, "Carlos, can you give an injection?"

Remembering his class in first aid at the Vocational Bible Institute, Carlos replied bravely, "Yes, I can."

The Colombian raced back through the jungle to Gilgal, and within two hours returned with a snakebite kit.

First, Carlos prayed for divine assistance. He knew that the future gospel work in that tribe depended upon the results. This was his first time to administer an injection. After the chief gave permission, Carlos prepared the hypodermic needle. As the injection was given, the Christians gathered around Gabriel, praying that the God of heaven, the Father of the Lord Jesus Christ would spare the boy's life.

Now the Indians saw a miracle. Never before had any of their number lived after being bitten by a snake. But this "Christian medicine man," Carlos Oliveros, had strong medicine. As the hours passed, young Gabriel still lived. Within days he was almost in normal health. The Indians recognized that here was greater power than their gods had ever shown. But when the light shines in the darkness that has been gathering for centuries, how slowly it penetrates.

However romantic and glamorous a visit to an Indian village might seem, Florence soon discovered that she must risk and conquer many obstacles on a life-and-death basis.

When Margaret Brabon and her ten-year-old son, John Mark, accompanied Florence on such a trip, after the plane flight to Turbo, they spent the night in their hammocks. Then, at four-thirty A.M. they trekked to the muddy docks to take a motorboat across the Gulf of Uraba. On the other side of the Gulf, they entered the Atrato River, and the boat made its way through the timbers floating down from logging camps.

Suddenly the lagoon ended, the river narrowed, and they were surrounded by the breathtaking beauty of the jungle. After one trip in the jungle Florence wrote, "Now I find myself surrounded by all the sounds and sights of the primitive wilds—foliage so dense, so high, so entwined, and so full of thorns that one cannot walk without cutting every step with an ax or machete. Birds, big and little, flashing such splendor of color that one remains dazzled as they flit from branch to branch. From somewhere amid the greenness, come chatterings, shrieks, grunts, the rustling of leaves, and the crackling of twigs by scurrying feet on the jungle carpet. A splash, a *blub,* a ripple tell us that the waters are alive also."

The three people were rudely awakened to reality as the boat stopped: it could go no farther in the shallow water, nor was any suggestion apparent as to how they could continue. They were on their own. As Florence and Mary contemplated the ankle-deep mud, the wonder grew as to how they could carry their luggage over such terrain. To their great relief, a dugout soon approached and offered to pole them upstream. This ended all too soon, and they had to get out and clamber up a steep bank toward a knoll, where they could try to organize their things. The two Indian boys who accompanied them, students at the Vocational Bible Institute, Florence, Margaret, and John Mark got their duffel bags and knapsacks on their backs, and started on fighting desperately to keep their balance in the deep slippery ooze of the trail. The new tennis shoes the missionary group wore were soon heavy as lead with mud. They dared not stop to rest, for the Indian boys pushed on ahead at a terrifying pace. Later they learned that the Indians had slowed down to half their usual speed to accommodate them!

At a little place called Unguia, where they got crackers and sausage to eat, they found some Kuna Indians who were glad to accompany them. As the missionary group started on once more, their heavy packs seemed to crush their aching muscles; but ahead of them, a small Indian girl gracefully tripped along over mud and stones, nonchalantly carrying five gallons of kerosene on her back!

At last they reached the chief's thatched-roof house where

they refreshed themselves with large, welcome glasses of lemonade. Then they bathed in the river only a few yards away. The naked children wore strings of beads around their necks, the men necklaces of alligator or monkey teeth, and the women elaborate beads brought from Panama. Everyone was busy cooking, sewing, or weaving beautiful baskets from reeds soaked in the river.

Florence showed pictures and told the gospel story. One young woman wanted her sins forgiven and voluntarily gave up the box of little idols under her hammock. Most seemed to have no comprehension of the message.

Florence already knew many words and phrases in the Kuna language. The Indian chief knew Spanish; so later in the evening, Florence and the chief worked over a tape recorder capturing a gospel story in the Kuna dialect. As they worked, the night noises from the jungle furnished a background along with tunes from Indian bamboo flutes, and the Indian conversation and laughter between the hammocks.

Later, a furlough in the States gave Florence an opportunity for linguistic study at one of the Wycliffe summer institutes. Upon her return to Colombia, she visited Dr. Weber, director of Wycliffe Colombian headquarters at Loma Linda. He praised the work Florence had already done in beginning a dictionary and a grammar of the Kuna language. He agreed that the Wycliffe translators would not only sponsor her and endorse her work, but keep a radio contact with her as they would with any one of their own workers, reviewing and guiding her work. It was an unusual tribute to Florence's ability and hard work.

As a further indication of success, the Kuna chief built an Indian house for Florence with two rooms, in one of which some Indian girls would live and work at hammock weaving.

Of course there were difficulties, and outside influences sought to turn the chief against the Christian religion. Life here was not easy. Half the year torrential rains made the ground a quagmire and travel almost impossible. When the wild storms drove in from the Atlantic, the trip back and forth across the Gulf of Uraba was dangerous.

The night before one return trip, Florence could not sleep. She repeated one verse of scripture after another, searching for a promise on which she could rest. At last Isaiah 41:10 came to mind, "Fear thou not; for I am with thee. Be not dismayed; for I am thy God. I will strengthen thee; yea, I will help thee; yea, I will uphold thee with the right hand of my righteousness." Now she could sleep.

The storm was so terrible that Florence and her fellow passengers had to wait all night in a thatched shack that, under the impact of the wind, threatened to disintegrate. Next morning, despite the storm, the pilot of the old battered motor launch announced their departure, and they started the trip down the Atrato River out into the Gulf of Urabá.

After an hour, they should have reached the port of Turbo, but the pilot had to admit he was lost amid the huge waves. Two and a half hours later he spotted land and attempted to go ashore, but the crashing waves against the rocky coast made that suicide. After three hours, the gasoline was running very low. If the motor stopped, it meant death upon the rocks or being swept out to sea.

Florence wrote of this, "I was pleading the promises God had given me and praying that, if necessary, He would make that motor run on air instead of gasoline!" The pilot had not the slightest notion where he was. Disaster seemed imminent and inevitable, when suddenly the boat rounded a jutting point of land, and Florence caught a glimpse of the port. Next day this same motorboat sank in the ocean and all on board were lost. God had indeed upheld that craft with the right hand of His righteousness. It takes good stuff to be a pioneer missionary.

For a time, another chapter opened to Florence. Adoption of Theological Education by Extension by the United Biblical Seminary of Colombia precipitated a crisis for the mission. The preparation of programmed texts for an increasing number of subjects was urgent. True to the remarkable pattern of her life and revealing a versatility that most must envy, Florence plunged into Spanish literature work.

But, after all, "the call of the wild" was too strong. For a time the Wycliffe Translators loaned a missionary couple to work among the Kunas. A young man of the tribe, training at the Vocational Bible Institute also assisted in evangelistic work. But more and more Florence has returned to this labor of love among people so long denied the gospel. One of the missionary heartaches in a field filled with opportunities is that the missionary is only one person.

Ask Florence Cavender if she thinks that mission fields no longer offer thrilling frontiers.

22

Still the Voice Cries, "Climb!"

IGNACIO GUEVARA, a roistering, carousing soldier in the Colombian army, was among those sent to restore and keep order for the Mission of the Andes when their Bible Institute at Garagoa was dynamited.

This young man Ignacio had gone so far in sin, his condition as a hopeless victim of alcohol seemed so desperate, that he decided to commit sucide—though he had little relish for that escape route. He was studying books on poisons to determine the quickest and easiest way out of a world where pleasure-seeking resulted in such a hell as he knew. But while guarding the Bible Institute, he was marvelously converted and transformed into a servant of the living God.

God works swiftly in some lives. Before long, Ignacio had become a Christian worker in Bogotá and began to visit relatives by the name of Cañon. The parents, though of the well-to-do professional class, accepted the gospel as did their son Carlos.

As a member of a cultured family, Carlos had educational advantages denied to many. He lacked only two years of graduation from high school, which in Colombia confers the A.B. degree.

But the urge of the Spirit was too great. Carlos had been converted under a man whose heart was on fire, a man who had evangelized on the gospel launch *El Cruzado.* The vision of his country's needs was so vivid that Carlos determined to leave school and enter Christian work. He volunteered to go wherever needed and was sent to open a new Christian day school in a river community that never before had known reading and writing.

Two months after beginning this school, the jaws of the law closed upon Carlos and his work. The missions' treaty was invoked and enforced, the school was closed and sealed, and Carlos was ordered to leave the vicinity immediately or face arrest on sight. Such an order could mean the application of the *ley de fuga,* according to which a prisoner is shot while (reportedly) attempting to escape.

Rage and sorrow that Colombia could deny schooling to its children because of partisan passions left Carlos weeping, as he bade adios to his rugged, ragged students.

Carlos managed to escape arrest until Gene Wittig came by with the launch, picked him up, and hid him under the aluminum flooring, down in the bilge of the launch, and took him to safe territory. Denied an opportunity for Christian service as a teacher, Carlos returned to Bogotá and completed his high school studies.

After graduation Carlos went to the Bible seminary in Medellin. There he met a man after his own heart, Dr. William A. Gillam, then seminary president. Bill Gillam set Carlos' heart aflame with a desire for more education. Some might ask, "Why can't a man like Bill be more careful about how hot a fire he kindles in a promising Colombian's heart?"

Carlos Cañon was now so hungry for learning that he went to the States. Some missionaries regarded going to the United States more or less as spiritual suicide; for many Colombians who went there remained permanently, where life is more pleasureful and where material comforts abound. Today, missionaries realize that highly trained Colombians of spiritual power may be the only key to future permanence of their work.

Carlos' experiences in the United States were somewhat like those of a missionary in reverse. He said, "I had learned English—studied it in high school in Bogotá. But not the rapid-fire kind I encountered in the USA. I would say, slowly, a word at a time, 'Would—you—please—say—that—again—more—slowly?' They might repeat it more slowly but still run all the words together. Then I would plead, 'More slowly!' until they were talking to me as though I was a child. Sometimes they talked to me as though I was an idiot, and sometimes I wondered if I wasn't an idiot!"

When Carlos fell in love with a gracious young lady born and bred in the United States, it indeed seemed that he was about to remove himself permanently from the Colombia field. If previously his return to Colombia had seemed doubtful, such a marriage as this seemed certain to bind him to North Amercia. Some people warned Carlos of the dire result of such a union, but Carlos was a rather strong-minded young man—he married the girl.

To pay for college, Carlos clerked in a store. It is probably impossible for the average American citizen to know how humiliating and shameful work is for a Colombian, if he is of a good family and can avoid such disgrace. But necessity is the mother of invention. Also the environment of America made it easier. Carlos himself said, "The grocery business put me through college. It also taught me that one is not worthy until he has worked."

When he married, financial needs increased. He added to his work load by teaching in the Berlitz School of Languages. Overnight this made Carlos a "professor" in a field that he commanded with ease. While doing advanced work at Washington University, he taught Spanish to Peace Corps men and women who were headed for Latin America.

Before he knew it, Carlos was language coordinator for the training program of the Peace Corps. He made schedules, trained teachers, reported on student progress. He became one of two men in the entire Pacific Coast area authorized to give Spanish language examinations to Peace Corps' workers. His technical and cultural studies included an analysis of the educational system in Latin America. Of course, with such success and prosperity, some thought he was utterly ruined for the mission field. Colombia would have to write him off. Who could expect him to leave such a career?

But, after all, there *is* God!

A reshuffling of the Peace Corps left Carlos without employment. Shortly thereafter, Bill Gillam spoke at a missionary convention in Seattle. Carlos attended. As he listened to his friend and teacher of past years, he heard the clear, robust voice of Christ calling him. God's ten-year program of training was complete, Carlos was prepared, and he was ready. Both he and his devoted wife, née Jane Hose, dedicated their lives to serve in the Inter-American Mission in Colombia.

What is just as amazing, they were both accepted by the board as missionaries—a Colombian had been made a missionary by an American board. But Carlos was an unusual missionary; he returned to Colombia in a dual role. He was a national who identified with all Colombians, and he was a missionary whose training and experience caused him to identify so perfectly with other missionaries that they forgot he was not a native American. A rare combination!

By this time, a task worthy of his preparation was awaiting Carlos in Colombia.

Carmen Hosma, converted in Segovia and baptized by Burton Biddulph in Barbosa, became a Christian day school teacher and went first to the fanatical and dangerous town of Colorado. She studied incessantly to be better prepared for her task. When she later became principal of the Christian day school at the Fourth Street Church of Bogotá, the number of students increased rapidly, until the rooms were incredibly crowded with laughing, loyal, lovable children.

By sheer personality, hard work, good planning—and some lobbying—Carmen got the school officially recognized by the Colombian government, and posted the official certification on a well-placed sign over the entrance to the Protestant church where the school operated. If anyone is inclined to doubt that this is a miracle, he does not know the Colombia of that day.

But Carmen had a vision beyond the day school that crowded Fourth Street Church to the bursting of its old three-foot thick adobe walls—something Colombia had not yet seen—a Christian high school!

At eighty years of age, Herbert Biddulph visited his son, Burton, in Bogotá. He had spent his life as a high school teacher and principal. He loved youth. His purpose in living was Christian education. By dint of frugality he had some life savings. The idea of a Christian high school in Bogotá captured his imagination. He furnished the money and purchased a strategic piece of land near the heart of the city—an ideal location for a high school. Soon one hundred eighty students were studying in a beautiful brick building. Burton was director of the mission. He had also been unanimously elected coordinator of the national campaign of Evangelism in Depth. When missionary Ben Perri, principal of the Christian high school received a grant for advanced studies that took him to the United States, Burton was obliged to assume this task also. Only a viking constitution and the heart of a saint gave him the serenity to keep from cracking under the tripartite responsibility.

Burton said, "I ought not to be doing this work at our high school. A national should be running this school." How often gringo missionaries have said that, but where is a man to be found? The cry of missionaries today as always is for Colombians of spiritual stature and thorough training to take responsibilities. This time, God had such a man! As though divinely timed, Carlos appeared on the scene. He was uniquely prepared by education and by experience, and he understood the mission, the church, and the heart of Colombian youth.

Like a wearied Atlas, Burton eased the burden of the Bogotá Christian High School onto Carlos' more youthful shoulders. This young man reveled in the work. For him it was a delight to assume such responsibilities. He was accustomed to the problems of faculty, curriculum, registration, student relations, discipline—all that makes a school a microcosm of an adult's strenuous world.

While Carlos was training in America, changes were taking place in Colombia as well. In 1958, Alberto Lleras Camargo ended *la violencia* when he became president. Violence was sharply reduced, and political conditions began to improve.

A letter from the Biddulphs dated October 14, 1969, gave glimpses of some thrilling things at Bogotá Christian High School since Carlos took over, things that cannot happen in Colombia but *are* happening.

"A Bible class is held in the big general hospital (a government institution) with posters in every ward announcing the Christian film to be shown. Carlos Cañon, our new principal in the Christian high school, made the contact. Over one hundred attended last week. High school students help bring the patients from the different wards and make posters with silk-screen process."

In *Colombia*?

In Colombia!

In a *government* hospital?

A government hospital!

Public evangelical meetings? Surely not!

Yes, you read it correctly.

Another unheard of thing—some high school students are acknowledging a divine call to the gospel ministry! Now God will have men capable of pastoring the developing city churches which are beginning to fill with professional people, college professors, and others of the intelligentsia.

To find God's Spirit working in the almost impenetrable strata of secondary education in Colombia is like seeing granite mountains melt.

Carlos Cañon's story proves that when a Colombian youth climbs the rugged pathway toward the heights, he lifts up with him all that a Christian mission exists for.

And, across Colombia's heat-drenched jungle lowlands and her chilling Andean heights, still the voice cries, "Climb!"

23

"Incredible! Fantastic! Miraculous!"

It was again Christmastime in Medellin. A quarter of a century had passed since our first Christmas here.

Tonight, upon the black bulk of the Andes that surrounded us, myriad dots of light showed where cabins and homes perched precariously on notches cut in the sheer slopes.

In the floor of the valley, the sea of sparkling lights almost seemed reflections of the starry canopy overhead. The Medellin we first knew had now trebled to over a million people. Toward the west, former pasturelands had been subdivided and covered with homes, except the land on which a modern airport accommodated the large jets. Eastward down the valley, I could see the lights of the Alliance for Progress homes on the south slope, and on the opposite slope the lights of homes that individual owners were slowly building on their own plots of ground. An "almost free" freeway now ran from east to west the length of the valley.

We took a ride in the mission car to downtown Medellin. We found that many of the narrow streets of yesteryear had become well-paved boulevards. Throngs of well-dressed people jostled on the commodious sidewalks; beautifully decorated plate glass windows invited late shoppers to make last-minute purchases. Merchants had learned the frenetic commercial ways of Babylon in the North. Only older citizens could remember the easygoing Christmas holidays that used to turn off the city of Medellin. Whether for gain or loss, those days were gone forever.

Towering trees still lined La Avenida and filled the plazas. Never had we seen them so gay. Prodigal quantities of electric lights—not Christmas miniatures—but large-sized light bulbs of every hue and color hung upon the trees in such profusion as though to atone for the drabness of bygone days.

Light, a spectrum of light, rainbows of light, poured down from these myriad bulbs. As brilliant, as colorful a Christmas spectacle, each of us vowed he had never seen before. Whether in streets or plazas, every leaf on every tree seemed to have become incandescent. Floods of light from the trees drenched everything in glowing color. Medellin had become a Christmas fantasy.

As we strolled through Bolívar Plaza, the radiant trees gave almost daylight splendor to the courts and walks. High in the air, immortalized in stone as in the hearts of his countrymen, Simón Bolívar still skillfully held rein on his fiery steed; and both shone against the huge mass of La Metropolitana, a brick cathedral, whose towers were faintly outlined with strings of wee lights, as though to say, "We too are still here." On the front terrace of the cathedral, shepherds worshiped about a somewhat neglected manger scene.

The real action was near the central fountain in the plaza where, with an accordion and a guitar, a group of Evangelicals had gathered a crowd. Hymns and Christmas carols preceded a gospel song composed by Colombians for Colombians, and brought to the listeners the authentic minor tune and the elusive lilt of Latin music.

Members of the group then passed out Spanish gospel tracts among the dense crowd. The men took them respectfully and many began reading them. Our missionary group, standing on the fringe of the crowd, also took tracts from the smiling Colombian who called us "brother."

Soon a Colombian opened his Bible and preached Jesus, of whom the angel prophesied, "He shall save his people from their sins." The message of the Word, throbbing with the love of God, pulled on hearts. You could feel the assent of those present.

We looked up at the shadowy immensity of La Metropolitana Cathedral, mute, almost abandoned tonight. Was this the Medellin of twenty-five years ago? Were these the Colombians of that bygone day?

No! In *this* Medellin, *this* Christmas, under the splendor of the city's Christmas lights, Colombians, unaided, unabetted by mission or missionaries, were evangelizing throngs of Colombians who listened intently to the good news of great joy to all people. No policeman kept order; none was needed.

Now I understood what Dr. Jose D. Fajardo, Cumberland Presbyterian, and noted evangelical leader of Colombia meant when he almost shouted, "What God's doing in Colombia is *incredible, fantastic, miraculous!*"

In the freedom of a new Colombia, under the Christmas splendor of this hour, in Bolívar Plaza in the city of Medellin, the Lord our Saviour had Colombians who were ready and willing to speak for Him. In them God "went by" on the Colombian road, winning hearts and lives to His service.

24

"Sound of a Mighty Wind"

NOT SINCE 1536, when Quesada's conquistadores captured The Gray City, capital of the Chibcha Indian tribe, and renamed it Sante Fé de Bogotá, had this metropolis seen anything so astounding.

Colombia's leading newspaper, *El Tiempo*, in its issue of Monday, December 16, 1968, carried the story under the caption, "Evangelicals Highlight Religious Liberty Existing in Nation." The article began, "Thirty thousand Evangelicals yesterday marched through downtown Bogotá."

In the accompanying photograph one could look down Seventh Street and see marching thousands moving toward Bolívar Plaza. The first of many banners seen in the picture carried the words, "The blood of Jesus Christ, his Son, cleanseth us from all sin"; the second, "Ye must be born again."

These marching thousands sang "A Mighty Fortress Is Our God" and "Onward, Christian Soldiers!" Many men held an open Bible high in the air above their heads. This truly was their sword, their banner, their ensign, their emblem, their watchword, their victory.

Sidewalks along the line of march were thronged. Some looked on curiously, seeking to read the banners; others listened, trying to understand the words of the songs.

The Bogotá march had been preceded by seven hundred thirty-eight evangelistic services, nineteen zonal interdenominational united crusades, and sixteen parades in larger cities. Youth and women's conventions had been held; medical, nursing, and dental caravans to poverty-stricken areas had been organized and sent forth, backed up by radio and television.

To climax such a prodigious national program of evangelism, Christian leaders from all parts of Latin America converged on Bogotá. First came intensive evangelistic campaigns in local churches. Then, for ten nights, the final crusade centered in the largest covered auditorium of the nation, Exposition Coliseum.

In the late afternoon, an hour before the crowds started pouring into the Coliseum, two hundred counselors met for a prayer meeting. The greatest international team of musicians, singers, and speakers ever assembled in Colombia brought crowds that taxed the ten thousand seating capacity of Exposition Coliseum. Paul Finkenbinder, beloved in both Americas, was the featured evangelist.

Each morning of the Bogotá crusade, pastors and Christian leaders crowded the Pan American chapel in a nine to twelve o'clock prayer meeting. At this gathering, Robert Lazaer distributed to pastors hundreds of decision cards filled out in the counseling room the previous night. Never had pastors faced so great a challenge as the follow-up of those making decisions for Christ.

One delight of this crusade was the presence of the three field directors, Pearson, Gillam, and Biddulph, whose combined years of service spanned the entire life of The Inter-American Mission in Colombia. They still met in the camaraderie of the days when they served together on the field executive committee—the same mutual respect, esteem, and Christian love that during the years had never wavered. Of these, Burton Biddulph, as coordinator of the Evangelism in Depth campaign was a national figure in this triumph of all that evangelical missions had previously accomplished in Colombia.

The high moment of the morning prayer services came with Bill Gillam's exposition of Jesus as seen in the book of the Revelation. He showed us the effulgent, eternal Christ walking in the midst of the seven golden candlesticks, holding in His hands the seven stars, the pastors of His churches (Rev 1:14-16, 20). He portrayed Jesus, the Lamb, in the midst of the throne of God, "as it had been slain," and the multitude singing, "Thou wast slain, and hast redeemed us to God by thy blood out of every kindred, and tongue, and people, and nation; And hast made us unto our God a kingdom of priests, and we shall reign on the earth" (Rev 5:6, 9-10). He revealed to us heaven opened and He who "was called Faithful and True . . . clothed with a vesture dipped in blood; and his name is called The Word of God," who rode at the head of "the armies that were in heaven," as "King of Kings, and Lord of Lords" (Rev 19:11, 13, 14, 16).

After one of Dr. Gillam's morning addresses, when the glory of the divine presence was very real, Rev. Ignacio Guevara, now the leader of an indigenous mission and church, arose, his face bathed in tears, and with deep emotion said, "We must have Bill Gillam in Colombia to serve the entire church of Jesus Christ. Will all who feel this, stand with me and pray that *Don Guillermo* shall be released to come to us!" The sincerity of the spontaneous and united prayer that followed was a heavenly seal upon the life and ministry of a man who had moved all whom he touched toward the knowledge and service of Christ.

In this moment the mission of the church in sending

Bill Gillam to Colombia had come full circle. The Colombia church, originally established by missionaries but now largely on its own, was requesting that the services of missionary Bill Gillam be made theirs by returning him to Colombia that Colombian Christians "might be properly equipped for their service" (Eph 4:12, Phillips). This too was part of the victory march of the church of the living God in Colombia.

Now, as the Bible Parade culminated in Bolívar Plaza, the nationwide Evangelism in Depth campaign in Colombia came to the highest peak of civic expression. Delegations from many parts of Colombia, the marching church groups of Bogotá, and thousands of friends demonstrated here that a tremendous, spiritual, revolutionary force was at work in Colombia. *This* revolution preached loyalty to the government and total surrender to God and to His Christ, plus love—always love—for everyone. Here was truth to create harmony in heart and home, to heal a nation which, in years past, had wounded itself so deeply by yielding to savage hatreds.

With unusual insight, the article in *El Tiempo* concluded, "The orator cried for Christian unity." Then the reporter added, "They seek for unity around Jesus."

> "Jesus," oh, how sweet the name!
> "Jesus," ev'ry day the same;
> "Jesus," let all saints proclaim
> Its worthy praise forever.

As the wreath-laying ceremony at Bolívar's statue officially ended the EID campaign, national recognition for the Evangelicals came from an unexpected source. President Lleras Restrepo, who evidently had been watching and listening, now came from the Presidential palace to mingle with the crowd, then walked to the capital steps, and shook hands with the leaders. History had never recorded such an incident as this in Colombia.

In the New Testament story of the primitive church, we read of "a mighty rushing wind." It seemed that God's winds were now blowing mightily upon these Colombian heights. Was a national, a continental, Pentecost to follow?

At the conclusion of this campaign, an internationally known Latin American evangelist, Santiago Garabaya, remarked, "Colombia is the greatest harvest field in Latin America. Colombia is the heart of evangelism today in Latin America."

Could this be the Colombia that the Inter-American Mission entered twenty-five years before? Could this be the Colombia of *la violencia?* Could the coordinator of so unparalleled an event in Colombian history as the EID campaign be the same Burton Biddulph who, counting his life forfeit, stood amid the threatening *puñaletas* in Envigado?

Paul Finkenbinder, whose radio ministry and evangelistic campaigns in English and Spanish have blessed thousands throughout the Western Hemisphere, said of the Bogotá campaign, "This is not only reaping but also sowing. This great campaign is only a crowning event following sorrow due to persecutions in the years of *la violencia*, and is but the firstfruits of a fabulous time of reaping."

Then he gathered up the spirit of the Evangelism in Depth campaign, and the spirit of the missions and the churches of Colombia, as he quoted:

What care I who gets the credit?
Only let the work be done:
God Himself will handle credit
At the setting of the sun!

Addendum

HEADLINES AND HIGHLIGHTS

THE ESTABLISHMENT of a foreign mission field not only blesses the people to whom missionaries are sent, but the society that thrusts them forth.

From the Inter-American Mission, founded in Colombia in August 1943, have come five members of the board of directors of the Oriental Missionary Society who were elected in the following order:

Benjamin H. Pearson
William A. Gillam
John Palmer
G. Burton Biddulph
Eugene A. Wittig

Two of these were given offices of worldwide responsibility:

Dr. William A. Gillam, was named vice-president in charge of deputation in the United States, and later became vice-president-at-large for world evangelism; and Rev. Eugene A. Wittig, vice-president of field ministries, became responsible for each of the mission's eleven fields.

Members of the Colombian evangelical churches in 1943 numbered approximately 3,000. By 1960 these had grown to 30,654 baptized members; and by 1966, these had increased to 63,810, with a total Protestant community of 255,240. In reciting this phenomenal growth, Ben Perri added, "The overwhelming fact is that the Colombia of the 1960s has experienced an actual revolution of religious attitudes—attitudes that spell opportunity." Today there are one hundred thirty congregations from the work begun in 1943.

Persecution has not destroyed but strengthened the church; enemies found that you cannot put out a fire by scattering it.

Recognition must be given to John XXIII, Pope from 1958 to 1963, for the apparent changes of attitudes and relationships in the Roman Catholic church.

On the Inter-American Mission field, the stepping-stones into this new Colombia may be found in headlines and highlights from reports of these years, which show that while tides may change, storm waves continue.

1957

The twelfth Victorious Life convention brought to the seminary campus Dr. Frederic Huegel, writer and orator from Mexico; musician Gene Jordan from HCJB radio, Ecuador; and Ruth Bergert, flutist. No newspaper articles, advertisements, radio announcements, nor handbills were permitted.

So great had become the popular hunger for the Bible that, amazingly, the Roman Catholic churches of Medellin announced September 30 as *Bible Day!* A newspaper editorial said, "Protestants have made us realize that the Bible is an inexplicable void to us Catholics. . . . The most ignorant believer among the Protestant sects studies it asiduously, moving among its many verses with ease. The astounding majority of us are ignorant of the Bible."

The Roman Catholic church even published a new family Bible at an unbelievably low price.

1958

River churches were reopened. These included the villages of Mexico, Galindo, and Colorado. VBI students from these towns went back as pastors.

On December 28, in the river town of Zaragosa, Harold Brabon dedicated a new concrete sanctuary built by former seminary student Jose Rodriguez. The previous church building had been burned in a riot.

1959

Businessman Eldon Turnidge and nineteen-year-old college student Dave Graffenberger from the United States arrived at the Vocational Bible Institute on January 14 to begin contour plowing with a tractor that Turnidge had bought and shipped down.

Three days later school ended for the fifty-three students. Burton Biddulph presented diplomas to five graduates. Gene Wittig was director of the institute and farm manager. A three-day Interdenominational Youth Congress followed. Then delegates arrived for the Inter-American Church Assembly.

Burton Biddulph, field superintendent since Bill Gillam was made director of deputation in the United States in 1956, was elected to the board of directors on July 1.

In November, a representative of World Vision approved the erection of a tabernacle for holding pastors' conferences on the seminary grounds at Manantiales.

1960

On April 2, ground was broken for the foundation of the new World Vision Tabernacle, one hundred feet long, fifty feet wide, and thirty feet high. A week of scrounging for cement had produced only one sack! After special prayer, twenty carloads arrived the following Monday! In one day Harold Brabon got four hundred sacks. Gene Wittig, in charge of building operations, put on day and night crews. The last slab of cement was poured May 7, to complete what, for Colombia, was a miracle building operation.

On Easter Sunday, April 17, Mrs. Charles E. Cowman, only living link with the founding days of the Oriental Missionary Society, author of the devotional companion to millions, *Streams in the Desert,* "took the last step" up "the hill which God desireth to dwell in," and began her work "from the Other Side."

On May 9, five weeks after beginning construction, three hundred thirty-nine representatives from twelve countries and twenty-eight denominations came by horseback, dug-outs, bus, railroad, and airplane to attend the first World Vision pastors' conference in South America. Local churches loaned benches, piano, and PA system.

The conference team included Dr. Bob Pierce; Dr. Paul Reese; Dr. Richard Halverson; Dr. Kyung Chik Han of Korea; W. C. Jones, businessman of Los Angeles; and concert marimbist, Jack Conner.

Rev. Robert Lazaer, Presbyterian missionary and executive secretary of the Evangelical confederation of Colombia, wrote, "This pastors' conference is one of the most significant events which has occurred in the one hundred four years of the Protestant church in Colombia."

Bill Gillam, in an article, added, "The huge tabernacle on the Medellin compound has already become a recognized convention center and a crossroads for intermission fellowship. The Inter-American Missionary Society is truly on the highway through Latin America." (The Pan-American Highway passed within two hundred feet!)

Increased facilities at the Vocational Bible Institute gave enrollment to eighty-one of the two hundred applicants. Eighteen graduated.

Thousands came to evangelistic campaigns in Bucaramanga and Barranquilla! Unheard of in Colombia! After an evangelistic tour in Colombia, Bill Gillam wrote, "I could well believe that the Colombian evangelical community was the fastest-growing church in the world, and that these Latin lands constitute one of the ripest harvest fields of the gospel."

At the Vocational Bible Institute, Gene Wittig brought the challenge, "Our mission in Colombia must raise up at least one hundred pastors and one hundred teachers during the coming two years if we are to take advantage of the opportunities open to us for spreading the gospel."

1961

The hidden river village of Caño Largo, evangelized by volunteers from Galindo since 1954, this year began supporting a student pastor from the Vocational Bible Institute.

The Colombian Inter-American Church Association paid fifty-five percent of all operating costs of their seventeen organized churches.

Bill Gillam was elected vice-president of the Oriental Missionary Society.

Margaret Brabon reported, "Five years ago one did not dare give a tract nor sell Bibles in public; today there is liberty. Three missionaries with twelve nationals covered the town of Puerto Berrio with a literature campaign. In two days they sold over three thousand scripture portions."

1962

The Interdenominational Christian Day School begun three years ago by the united evangelical churches of Medellin reported enrollment increased from thirty-three to one hundred seventy-five. The IMS established a boarding department for children from other cities.

Ben Perri observed, "Everytime a Colombian believer enters a train, some type of witnessing goes on. Never have I seen such a witnessing church nor such a witnessing laity."

Boots, boats, and bullets! Florence Cavender traveled with a seminary quartette to evangelize river areas. The floods were so high, people had to paddle up the streets in their canoes to reach the church! In some villages all but the thatched roofs disappeared in the muddy waters.

1963

Carol Harding stopped at Pedro Pablo's "Lighthouse" on the river to hold a children's meeting. Pedro had wanted the *El Cruzado* gospel launch to stop at his poor little shack, but later he found some believers and asked them to send him someone to teach him. Martin Echeverri went and led him to accept Christ as Saviour. In gratitude, Pedro built this rough "lighthouse" chapel, and invited his friends to come and pray. Here, as always, Carol charmed the children and their elders with her illustrated stories.

As supervisor of elementary Christian day schools, Mildred McCary spent hours in a motor-driven dugout, rode a mule on a crude packsaddle, walked six miles through the mountains, then bedded down for the night on the dirt floor of a "hotel." She felt uneasy as a drunk man came in with a lady companion to share the same floor; but she prayed, then: "Fear not, I will strengthen thee; yea, I will help thee," and she fell asleep from weariness. Why would a young lady prefer to do this rather than anything else in the world? Because "sixty percent of primary-age children had no education," and the love of Jesus constrained her.

Carmen Hosma, orphaned at twelve years of age, converted in Segovia, and baptized at Barbosa, in 1958 became director of the Bogota Elementary Christian Day School. The forty pupils with which she began, this year became one hundred ninety pupils, absolutely crowding out the old church building.

Ben Perri's greatest thrill came in dedicating a new church in the heart of the jungle with one hundred fifteen people present. The church was the first building in the new frontier town of Gilgal in northern Colombia, near the border of Panama. Ernesto Durango from Sopetran was leader. Two other Christian laymen joined him. From their witness came this church. The next building planned was for the pastor. The people requested a teacher for their children. They promised to pay all expenses and build the schoolhouse. Then they planned to build houses for themselves around the town square. Months at a time rain and mud isolated them from the outside world, but they put first things first.

1965

The one hundred fifty-member congregation in the river village of Colorado succeeded in erecting a third church building. Mobs had destroyed the first two by fire, so this time the members built with cement blocks. At ten o'clock one April night, four organized bands arrived with sledgehammers, crowbars, picks, knives, and guns, and completely razed the new construction.

But Colombia was different now. The nation reacted vigorously against this violence. Three radio reports expressed shock at this "savagery." The names of the mob leaders were published. Government commissions came to view the wreckage.

Now the beautiful new sanctuary with pink walls, Sunday school rooms, and a pastor's study, is the only church building open for services in Colorado. The traditional church ceased to function regularly for lack of interest.

1966

An Inter-American bookstore began in Medellin.

In December, in the cities of Cali, Medellin, and Bogota, immense united evangelistic campaigns took place in public buildings rent free, with radio, TV, and press coverage! Large evangelical parades marched unmolested through the downtown areas. The understatement of the year seemed to be, "Things have changed drastically." The only explanation: *God* changed things drastically!

1967

The long cherished dream of those beginning the teaching program of the Medellin Bible Seminary in 1944 was realized by adopting the name the *United Biblical Seminary of Colombia,* electing representatives of seven missions to the board of directors, with students from ten denominations.

Rev. Wallace Rehner, dean of the seminary, was elected Executive Secretary of Theological Education by Extension for Colombia, Ecuador, Venezuela and Panama, and the United Biblical Seminary was authorized to begin the program.

1970

In April, 1970, Wally and Betty Rehner were killed, along with their pilot Frank Tefft and his wife, in a plane crash near Lansing, Michigan.

1971

One June 29, 1971, William A. Gillam died of a malignant brain tumor in southern California at the age of fifty-seven.

The World Vision Pastors' Conference held in October under the auspices of the United Biblical Seminary of Colombia registered over eight hundred paid delegates with one thousand two hundred in attendance at the Medellin Civic Auditorium, use of which was granted free of charge.

A leading Catholic industrialist began attending Bible classes conducted by Harold Greenlee, of the United Biblical Seminary teaching staff, and in turn is conducting his own weekly Bible classes among friends and employees.

Rev. Burton Biddulph, rector of the United Biblical Seminary of Colombia, reported that the Theological Education by Extension program has increased enrollment to three hundred fifty-five students!

On November 3, Dr. Frederic J. Huegel died in Springfield, Illinois, at the age of eighty-two. Dr. Huegel had authored several books; the most recent was *The Ministry of Intercession.*

1972

Harold Brabon and his wife were on a deputation tour on February 24, when he suddenly slumped in the car seat and was gone. His final words to his daughter were about the ministry in Medellin. "Time is running out," he told her. "The Communists and false sects aren't sitting down waiting. Act while it is day."